THE GIFT

OF

THRIFT

A GUIDE TO USING FRUGALITY TO PROVIDE A
LIFE OF CLASS, SOPHISTICATION, & WEALTH.

BY BENJAMIN LOUGHRIN

This book is dedicated to my dad.

He taught me (among other things):

Waste Not Want Not,

A Penny Saved is a Penny Earned,

Money doesn't buy happiness,

and that creativity & money can be used

interchangeably

Table of Contents:

Introduction:

Poorer Than Before

My first book, *Retirement Arbitrage in Guatemala*, was about having a great life for pennies in beautiful Guatemala. While it might describe the most effective way of stretching more out of your money, most people aren't at all familiar with Guatemala and aren't nearly adventurous enough to uproot themselves and move to another country, and I can understand that.

Since covid, economic conditions globally have resulted in almost everyone everywhere having less disposable income than they did before covid. It would appear that the widest distribution of wealth might have been somewhere around late 2019, putting the height of civilization firmly in the rear-view mirror. The road ahead is filled with uncertainty, except of course that individually we would all be wise to pay closer attention to the way we spend money as to get the most out of its apparent dwindling supply. Technically, the supply is growing, causing inflation to reflect that it takes more money to get the same stuff than it did before, but unless you're making significantly more than you used to, you're poorer than you used to be.

The bright side would be that even being poorer than you used to be, if you're from the US, Canada, Europe, or any first world nation, you're still actually quite wealthy on a global scale and will probably make due just fine with a few adjustments. Typically speaking, the wealthier you are, the more money you waste. When all you have is a hammer, everything looks like a nail. Likewise, when you have money available to solve a problem, it's often easier to use money to solve the problem than to look for another solution. This isn't always a bad strategy, but if you're used to operating that way and money is now beginning to get tight, you could probably benefit from strategies to solve problems without throwing money at them.

The process of getting wealthier as you age is a wonderful and natural progression that most successful people achieve. We all remember ramen dinners in the early days of being out on our own, and the satisfaction of upgrading our meal selections as we progressed in our careers. Eventually you build a family and your obligations require you to provide more than you had done previously. Luckily as your experience grows so does your earning power and your obligations are met, even if sometimes by the skin of your teeth and with the help of some short term credit. Getting wealthier as you get older is perfectly natural, fulfilling, and generally fun as you get to decide how to spend the money you never used to have.

On the other hand, having less than you used to have is much less fun. For lots and lots of people, that's where we are now. We don't necessarily have less money, in fact we might even have more, but the spending power of the money has gone down thanks to inflation, leaving us in the end, with less.

Old habits die hard, and living with less is something that nobody enjoys. This is where people get into serious problems with credit card debt, digging themselves deeper into a depressing hole to maintain the living standard their dependents have become accustomed to. Debt would only be the correct approach if there was a reasonable assumption that conditions would change and return to normal within a brief timeframe. This would not appear to be the case.

If inflation was caused by the quantitative easing policy of printing trillions of dollars starting in 2020, look how long it took to actually catch up to marketplace pricing. It's late 2023 as I write this and the effects of inflation are perfectly obvious to everyone but the most blindly optimistic of us. It took until earlier this year for people to begin to even notice the change in buying power. Couldn't we therefore assume that the three year delay that it took to significantly affect prices, might be reflected on the other end? As in: if money printing policies stopped today (which they won't), wouldn't it take another three years to finally realize the real value of money compared to goods in the marketplace?

So in short, if you're feeling poorer now, just wait. It's highly likely to get even worse. I wouldn't hold out for any solutions from the government either. Given their most recent track record, they are much more likely to make it worse than to provide any type of solution. They too have been digging an ever deepening hole that stands to engulf the whole thing because nobody has the stomach to face the truth and tell the dependents that we can't keep spending like the way we have been in the past. Sound familiar?

I have a solution. Not for greater economic woes that will eventually and undoubtedly affect us all, sorry. My solution is for the individual who is lucky enough to live in a developed country and is probably spending way more than they need to as a result of habit, ego, and bad planning. Tame the Ego, change the habits, and plan ahead of time to get better value out of your money and your life in general.

This isn't a book about how you can squirrel away money by eating only oatmeal and living under a freeway bridge. It's about how you can live a full life with dignity and class, because remember: class is not about money, it's about education and the conviction to live the proper way. It costs way less than you think but it does require skills, commitment, and planning. Anyone can do it but they have to put their minds and hearts in the right place.

THE MINDSET

My Aunt, when she was young, went on a trip to Europe and ended up marrying a Frenchman. As I recall, the news of the proposal was a bit of a shock to the family but in the end, the union was made, the two were married, and our extended family now included a Frenchman.

His name was Jean Philip. They lived in Germany and would come to the United States to visit for important family events like weddings, funerals, or sometimes for no particular reason at all. On one particular visit Jean Philip made shrimp. I was something like 12 years old and didn't like seafood at the time, except maybe fish-sticks (as a courtesy to my younger readers: fish-sticks were a frozen product made from mashed up fish parts, formed into sticks (like mozzarella sticks), breaded, fried, then frozen and boxed. They were then heated in an oven and served with tartar sauce or mayo or maybe ketchup.).

I was timid to taste the shrimp, perhaps partly because my uncle Ben always referred to shrimp as "the cockroaches of the sea", which even in retrospect, is approximately true. The smell was enticing and the present company encouraged me, so in the spirit of adventure and trying new things I skeptically peeled the shell with my inexperienced fingers and revealed the naked shrimp beneath. After a quick glance around the table to be sure I wasn't setting up to be the butt of anyone's joke, I placed the delicate morsel in my mouth and absorbed the sensory input from my tongue and mouth. I was pleasantly surprised. Quite so.

Butter, garlic, lemon, salt. Oh, yes, and shrimp. Amazing. This was a life changing moment. I took a risk and it paid off. Worst case scenario: I don't like it and I have to cleanse my palate with a few gulps of whatever might have been available. Best case: I begin a lifelong quest of enjoying the broad assortment of delicious ocean creatures and all the wonderful ways of preparing them. It wasn't just about seafood, it was about getting the most out of what was available. Making the best of things. If you could make cockroaches taste that good, I would consider eating them, just not in front of any French people.

French people have a reputation for being arrogant. Especially to Americans. Jean Philip was never that way, but nonetheless, he was very French. French people seem arrogant because they look at Americans like we are dogs. Or, that we eat like dogs. We have lots of money, but we have no taste. They make a clear distinction between having money, and having taste. Or class. To them, money is not class, which is correct.

We work all the time and don't take proper vacations. We have access to good things, but don't utilize them properly. We gulp our wine for its intoxicating properties instead of savoring its delicate flavors and understated qualities. We have a beautiful country, but we are too busy with our constant development so as to spoil its natural beauty. Americans view their houses, cars, and bank accounts as testament to their accomplishments. Frenchmen view their lives and adventures as their accomplishments. Part of me thinks they are right.

The French perspective is that there is a proper and correct way to live and to do things. Americans think about providing for the future. The French think about the moment they are living in now. Is the way I am living in this moment now correct? Have I done justice to the gifts I have received from god to make the most out of this exact moment? This is a typical latin trait. The same can be said for Italians, Spanish, Portuguese, Latin Americans (which makes me think it's something to do with the latin based language they all share). They honor god by enjoying his gifts so that he may enjoy his own creation through them and their experiences. Americans tend to sacrifice to provide for a generation not yet born. The French perspective is that Americans are throwing the baby out with the bathwater.

Asians are much like Americans in that sense, but even more so. Especially disciplined, particularly prepared to sacrifice, completely un-indulgent, and very much focused on providing well for the next generation. Asian Americans have done so well in America that their children have been sufficiently provided for as to soften and become less disciplined as to reflect the character of their American neighbors. Their parents were frugal savers, keen investors, shrewd in business, and diligent business owners; focused on providing well for their children, which they did with extraordinary success.

On the path to getting great value for money and likewise for life, we will adopt a philosophy somewhere in between the thriftiness of 1st generation Asian American immigrants with the value for experience of the French.

This amalgamation will put us in the mindset to find the best value according to: Lowest dollar amount spent for highest life value achieved. We will therefore subvert the ego, social pressure, societal pressure, and your old dumb tendencies that are keeping you from living a tasteful life within your actual means.

Avoid Egotistical Pursuits

Many people spend far too much time and money on trying to look rich rather than trying to become rich. While it feels great to wear nice clothes, drive nice cars, and enjoy incredible food at fancy restaurants; these things can keep you from elevating your position if you indulge beyond your means and for the wrong reasons. Ask yourself if you really need the things you want, or if you are just stroking your own ego. Most people grow big heads as their careers begin to take off and go wrong in three important categories: Cars, Clothes, Eating Out.

There are other categories in life that can be expensive like: cigars, golf, and bars; but these things are more like hobbies and can therefore be more easily avoided in the short term. Everyone needs a car, everyone needs to wear clothes, and everyone needs to eat. So it would seem that these things are bare necessities, which they are, but the degree to which you spend on these things is the important part. Cigars and bars are something that, while they might provide some networking opportunities, should generally be reserved for people who are already on track with all investment goals and still have too much money lying around. Golf is a bad one too, but the networking opportunities are more potent so I'd leave that one to your own personal discretion.

I'm not trying to spoil the fun because people get great pleasure out of cars, clothes, and fine food; but that's precisely the kind of thing we need to watch out for. If it feels good, watch out for those intoxicating effects. These types of indulgences creep their way into emotional places in your mind and justify themselves the way something boring wouldn't. They become so ingrained in your self image that quitting them or even slowing down can feel like an existential threat. The sooner you get onto the program of acquiring those things with a thrifty mindset the better because it's a nasty habit to try to kick.

There is a philosophy that exists that does have some merit: that a young person fresh in their career should go out and buy a new car because the practice of making the payments keeps them focused on their career and gives them discipline and makes them accustomed to make payments which can later be converted into making payments on a house. While I can agree with this in spirit because I respect the concept of cultivating a respect for setting money aside for payments instead of spending it on something frivolous, I would suggest one modification: buy a lightly used car on payments instead. So much value is lost when you drive a new car off the lot but more on that later.

The thrill of buying expensive things should be saved for later, when you can actually justify the expensive things you are buying. Instead, cultivate a taste for the thrill of the deal. The thrill of getting a good deal is a much less dangerous emotional response, but not completely without danger, which we'll talk about in detail later. If you spend your money trying to fulfill your ego, you'll find that your ego grows faster than your earning power. Throw credit cards into the mix and you'll be facing the same soul punishing incarceration-by-debt that millions of Americans feel trapped and oppressed by every day. Thrift is the vehicle that can keep you falling into that hole, and god forbid you are already in that hole, it's the only thing that can get you out of it.

The first step to getting out of or staying out of that kind of trouble is recognizing when you want to buy something because you have a practical need for it, or because it fulfills a desire from within your ego. This requires the utmost self honesty because your ego will undermine your conscious self with millions of justifications and shame you into splurging on things that are beyond your means. You must have a firm sense of self identity, and part of your identity needs to be based on a value for prudence.

If you can respect yourself as prudent, you can reflect on the prudence of a purchase during your decision making process. Your ego will be telling you all kinds of justifications, such as one of your friends or work associates already has one, or a friend or work associate will be jealous if you have one and they don't. Remember, your ego doesn't care about your long term situation because your ego is not prudent. Also consider that your friend or work associate that already has one may or may not be prudent, and might be in a different situation than you. Basing your decisions on the decisions of other people is neither logical nor wise. You have to live with your decision, so make sure you've run it through your prudence circuits before you buy.

The prudence judgment is a sound and sober voice of reason that logically asks the question: what is the minimum that I can get away with, and what's the maximum that I can afford. Your ultimate decision should be somewhere in the middle of these two. Let your prudence help you decide whether it's worth it to you to pay the difference between the minimum and the maximum, and at the very least avoid paying beyond your personal maximum. Have a system in place to help you make these types of decisions, and if you find yourself feeling any emotion at all during the decision making process, don't buy, just wait.

Most marketing and sales will eventually employ a sense of urgency to get you to buy before you come to your senses. 'While supplies last', or 'get yours before they're all gone', or 'for a limited time only'; all these phrases are commonly used to make you think that if you don't act in that exact moment, you'll miss out forever. They know that people shop with their egos and want to get you to buy before the more prudent part of you wakes up and stops the whole thing.

Have a few techniques ready to help you avoid impulse buys. Sometimes taking just ten minutes to go for a walk and think about it is enough to prevent you from making an impulsive purchase. If it's a big purchase, take the time to call the wisest person you know who knows you and cares about your situation and ask them if they think it's a good idea to buy. Go home and sleep on it. Talk to your husband or wife first. Take lunch and mull it over. Just don't let yourself make decisions impulsively. Avoid that one thing and you'll be ahead of the game.

Of all the things you feel tempted by in the moment, the vast majority will still be available a day later. If that's the case, throw that sense of urgency out of the window. If you've thought it over and still think it's a prudent buy, come back the next day and buy it. If it's no longer available, relax, now that you've already gone through the decision making process you'll be ready next time you see one. It's better to lose a couple scores than to buy things you don't need and can't afford.

A shopping addiction is like a gambling problem, there is no amount of money that can satisfy it. It has the potential to destroy marriages, families, and lives. Even if it's not particularly bad it still has the potential to put you in a dangerous position with debt, something that has horrible psychological consequences. It can manifest in many ways but in the end the ego is always the root cause. If you find yourself looking at something to buy, if your ego chimes in at all, beware. It doesn't matter what it says, the fact that it's speaking at all means it's time to stop and go the other way.

Everything you buy is a tool. A car is a tool of transportation and an object of status. Clothes are a tool to keep you covered and make you look the way you want to look. Eating in restaurants is a tool to demonstrate your class and sophistication. Emotion is not necessary when buying tools. When buying tools, you assess if the tool is sufficient to complete the job you are trying to complete. You might need a car that projects a certain degree of sophistication, if that's the case, make your decision with prudence to make sure you buy something that suits your needs while at the same time within your means. You'll enjoy the feeling you get when driving it if you know you didn't mess up your financial wellbeing to get it.

Transportation (Cars):

If you need a good looking car to appear professional in your field, the cost difference between a brand new car and a slightly used car is significant. The USA is a place with an abundance of wonderful vehicles, let someone else lose a large chunk of the value simply by driving it off the dealership lot. Your best bet at finding a good one is to not be in a hurry so you can take your time to find the right one. The most important factor when buying a used car is the attitude of the seller. Someone who is in a hurry to sell or sees the car as a burden to store is the ideal seller. Even better if they dislike the prospect of selling altogether. If they view that you're doing them a favor just by taking it off their hands, negotiations will go in your favor if you've got the gumption to whittle them down to their bare minimum.

As a younger man I had a negotiation turn out great for a car that I got many years of great use out of. There was a Subaru down the street from where I lived that had a for sale sign on it for several months. This was not a very well trafficked street so it was no wonder he hadn't had much interest in the car. I was in the position to buy a car because my work truck drank gas and I wanted something with better economy and more seating for the weekends and around town. The sign said $3500 obo. I was in a good negotiating position because I really didn't need the car, and I could tell by the low effort approach of the seller, that he was not only not very interested in selling cars, but that he was probably sick of looking at it taking up space in his driveway.

I called the number a few times and finally got a hold of the seller. Turns out the car used to be his late wife's car and had been given to his son, used during his college years to go back and forth from San Luis Obisbo to Tahoe, hence the high mileage. The son had moved on to something else and the father was left with the burden of selling the car. He was a lawyer and busy with some home renovation projects, and selling this car was hardly on his list of priorities. I knew if I offered too little, or had an unfavorable attitude he would refuse to sell it to me out of spite, but he obviously didn't have much of an interest in the car and viewed it as a burden more than anything else.

I told him I had $700 cash and could come up with more if he was willing to wait. He took the $700, gave me the title and washed his hands of the whole thing. That car was wonderful to me for years and never needed more than a battery, oil changes, and a change of tires the whole time I owned it. It eventually succumbed to a worn out clutch and I was ready for an upgrade so I traded in for my next car with the same indifference as the seller I bought it from. The moral of the story is that the attitude of the seller might be the most important factor in the purchase of a vehicle, or any commodity for that matter.

Now for me driving a $3500 car (or $700 depending on how you look at it) suited my needs just fine, it can't be assumed to work in all circumstances for all people. While the car had a clean body and in the end proved to be mechanically sound, it was clearly not a brand new or even late model car. It wasn't a beater, but it was hardly a source of personal pride. I had other sources for stuff like that.

I understand that not everybody is in a position to drive something that old without incurring some type of embarrassment. It is not a sin to not want to drive an older looking vehicle and I understand people have their reasons and criteria for choosing newer vehicles with warranties and guarantees and loaner cars in the event of mechanical problems. It depends upon your own situation and your comfort level and dependency on a 100% uptime vehicle.

Personally, I love cars like that because if somebody accidentally scrapes it with a shopping cart my blood pressure remains relatively unaffected and I don't like to invest emotion or stress into tools, which is effectively how I view vehicles in my own life. I also have mechanical abilities that allow me to take bigger chances with machines than someone without those skills. When I bought my first car my dad gave me a bag of basic tools to always have in the car with me in case of mechanical problems while on the road. I've made this an institution in all the cars I've owned since (all used). Those tools, plus my intermediate mechanical abilities, have allowed me to have transportation for a small fraction of its "new" or "like-new" cost. That's the value of those skills.

I don't think I'll ever buy a new car. It seems like such a waste to me. I can't imagine paying forty or fifty thousand dollars to have the expectation of reliability only to be roped into overpriced required maintenance at the dealership under the threat of losing my warranty if I take my car to a perfectly good mechanic who charges half of what the dealership would. Over the life of the car, all that required overpriced maintenance is a lot of money, in addition to the massive value difference between new and used. If a car will drive for 300k miles, I'd prefer to have it only for the last 200k, for which I'll probably pay a fifth of the price to own it, while receiving two thirds of it's value. Check my math but that's like a 10x value gain.

If you don't have the mechanical abilities, then the options will be different for you, but that doesn't mean that you can't save significantly on this most basic of expenses. I'm asking you to make your car buying decision with sober logic and not with emotion and ego. Yes you've been doing well at work, and yes you deserve something shiny and attractive. So get something slightly used, or factory approved pre owned. In either circumstance you'll save a bundle and no one will ever know the difference. There's ton's of outlets selling roadside assistance and plenty of good mechanics available if you ask around. Make your own guarantee.

Like most of the strategies in this book, it's only a matter of planning. Spend an hour calling mechanics in your area and find out who likes working on the brand of car you have. Stop by and introduce yourself and show the car you have or the one you are thinking of buying. The relationship of having a good mechanic whom you already know and knows you, is a better guarantee than the dealership guarantee that they guarantee that you will get fleeced every time you bring your car in. My secret to making your money go further does not mean you have to drive a beater car, it means that transportation is a significant expense in everyone's life, especially in the USA, and there are many opportunities to save if you put in the effort.

On par with gambling & crack cocaine: Clothes

As for clothes, you might be in the same predicament: maybe you need to dress well to inspire confidence in your professionalism. Dressing well does not mean having a shopping addiction and a collection of Louis V handbags. Simply questioning your own motivation can do a lot to curtail an expensive habit of over-consumption. If you like nice stuff and need it for your professional life, just limit the quantity and frequency of your purchases. Shop deals and buy quality with the intention of using it enough to eventually wear it out. Most people that love buying new clothes actually just love the act of buying, because it strokes their ego and fulfills their need to feel rich and successful. They'll find they overbuy, max-out their credit cards, and end up sending their past purchases to the thrift store, thus losing all of its value . The best value in clothes would be to buy it after the original owner has already lost all the value while the garments have retained all of their value as a result of either having never been worn or having been hardly worn at all. The funny thing is, the buying addiction often means, the nicer the clothes, the less they've been worn.

I know used clothing is somewhat of a taboo among people that view themselves as classy, but I'm willing to forgive ignorance as long as you've paid full price for my book. Often I find stuff at thrift stores that still have the tag. A good reason to get rid of a nice piece of clothing is because it doesn't fit. I've scored countless bargains, brand new, in thrift stores I can only assume for that exact reason. In Guatemala where my wife and boys live part of the year I've done the best, believe it or not. I'm pretty sure it has something to do with the fact that anything my size that ends up down there is simply too big for the bulk of the local population to utilize. I've scored local favorites like North Face, Patagonia, Columbia, Coto Paxi, Lulu

Lemmon, and more simply because I'm a size that's not common in those areas. Furthermore, I don't pay full price.

A thrift store in Guatemala is called a Paca. Pacas somehow get clothes from the US in Super-Sacks, giant bags the size of a pickup bed. When they open a new bag, some items will get cherry-picked, and everything else will be offered for sale for usually about 20Q. 20Q is about $2.60 in USD. Now, how could I consider myself qualified to write a book about stretching your money for a life of quality if I paid $2.60 USD for a $69 USD Patagonia shirt? Of Course I couldn't. After a week or so Paca's will put a sign out front that says "Todo 15Q". That's usually when the suckers rush in thinking they are getting a good deal. Another week goes by and it's "Todo 10Q". Amateurs. I generally wait till "5Q" before I even start looking. When the sign reads "2Q" or "1Q" I'll stop by and make sure I've brought my wallet. Since nobody is my size anyway, I'd be a fool to pay more than 2Q, right?

Some of you might be thinking that I've left money on the table by buying at 2Q instead of waiting for 1Q. Perhaps you are right. However, since 2Q is about 27 cents USD, some local buyers might buy even though it doesn't fit but instead just because it makes a larger rag, or could be made into a handsome pillow case. In some of these cases, if it's a good brand, still has the tag, a color or style I like, or in particularly good shape, I will buy it even though it is 2Q instead of 1Q (double the cost). It's one of those times you have to remind yourself it's about the value and not the cost.

Before you get all excited about the time investment required to find deals like this you have to understand that, like many strategies to living better with less put forward in the book, there is a system involved. The system is to do quick stops. To stop and look quickly only when it's convenient or serves some other purpose. For example: I often have business to take care of at the local copy shop. This business usually means I send an email ahead of time and then show up at one of their locations and ask them to process the order. This usually takes about 5 minutes, thus providing me the opportunity to step across the street and peruse the selection at the nearby pacas. Even if it's 20Q week I can still have a look at the inventory, and though I hate to admit, if there's something good for my wife or the boys, I'm not beyond paying 20Q for a quality garment if it meets my stringent criterion.

The trick is to move fast. One can't wander around all day when there are places to go and people to see. One must seize the day and take care of the pressing business of the moment. This is why I have the 5 Minute Rule. The 5 Minute Rule is best understood in the context of the United States, because time moves faster there. The trick is to drop in as frequently as possible to your favorite thrift stores in moments where you need to burn time anyway. Let's say you're waiting for a call, or have a few minutes before lunch break ends, or have to meet someone but it's not quite time yet (not a bad trick if you struggle being on time). This is an opportunity to do a Quick Pass walk-through.

You'll learn the layout of these places your first couple times though. You only want to go to the sections of interest based on what you might need at the time. A QuickPass is literally a fast walk, only in the places of interest, only looking at first for sizes (look at the length of shirt arms and pant legs) and then at brands as you find possible scores. Assess condition and quality and move on immediately if it doesn't jump out as a spectacular buy. If it's for you, then hold it up to see if it fits, if it does, ask yourself, "How often will I wear this?". If the answer is, "not very often", put it down and never look back. More on that later.

You don't need very many clothes anyway. Three generations ago ordinary people would have like 20 garments to their name, including underwear, if they were lucky. It's different now, so I guess you'll have to settle with the size of your closet.

The main problem with this approach is that in the land of plenty, you will inevitably run out of closet space. The bright side is that it's hardly costing you anything to do it. In the US it's costing you a dollar or two per garment, in Guatemala, approximately 7.65 times less. Not very much, but then again: waste not want not. In the instance where you have nowhere to put your awesome scores, you must apply this new criteria, just as you should have been doing the whole time: "Since I already have something like this, is this one good enough for me to retire the one I have to replace it with this?". If the answer is no, leave on the rack and leave before you have second thoughts.

THE MOST PROLIFIC MONEY KILLER: EATING OUT

There is hardly anything more enticing in this world than eating out every night, especially in a big city where options are plentiful, wonderful, and constantly changing. After just a month or two in a new city you're going to have a couple of favorites. Those will eat up most of the week. Fridays and Saturdays will be considered special and maybe warrant a new place or a special (expensive) old favorite. Breakfast burritos in the morning, Philly Cheesesteaks for lunch break, and the assortment of options for nights out, takeout, delivery, doordash, with the wife. You could dump $60k per year into this endeavor. This is not a good investment.

I have a cousin that lived in Los Angeles. He and his wife are not only very good looking people, but charming as well. I was visiting years ago and had the pleasure of staying with them. In the morning I was the first one up and went out to grab some eggs and such to make omelet for breakfast. Having just been to the store I was surprised and shocked to learn that they did not have any cooking oil in the house. No butter, no ingredients of any kind. There were boxes of takeout in the fridge. That's all.

"How could this be?" I silently thought to myself. "How do you cook?" I asked out loud.

"We do not cook," he replied.

My brain was rattled to a standstill.

"What do you mean you do not cook?" I stammered out.

"We go out." he replied.

At the moment I was unable to process the information. It slowly tumbled out of my makesenseikers and understandicles: they were saying that they do not cook at all. What could this mean? It must mean that they indeed do not cook at all. Meaning: no need to have a frying pan, a pot, a spatula, ingredients, or cooking oil. I was completely and utterly flabbergasted.

I made them omelet for breakfast, which in truth was of the amateurish type I didn't know any better than at the time (however it should be noted that there were particular challenges surrounding cooking in a kitchen without correct tools that had apparently never been cooked in before). Hardly competitive with the wonderful selection of restaurant omelets available in LA, they must have thought me a fool to muck around trying to cook for myself, especially for the purported "most important meal of the day".

Then I went on to offend his wife with my ridiculous opinions about this or that and the whole thing was wrapped up when I discovered a homeless person taking a crap in the stairwell of their apartment complex and I offered to be the bad guy and chase her off (surly out of guilt for producing such a mediocre omelet) which was also not particularly well received.

Earlier, before the homeless person, he revealed that he did not touch raw chicken. Not that he had never done it, just that he had resolved to never do it again. I was so confounded and befuddled that my brain resorted it's simplest of states, perhaps why I though my only source of value at the time was my willingness to chase off a homeless defecator, something in normal circumstances I would have had the social perceptive abilities to realize was not considered by my hosts as a valued contribution in the moment.

The trouble in this situation was that from their perspective, I could have only been found guilty of being stupidly cheap, tone-deaf, imposing, and with the homeless person: indifferent and mean. It wouldn't help that my ex who was with me at the time with our new baby, was a classless piece of work, and that the reason for our visit was that they had been married the night before. So perhaps their honeymoon omelett was spoiled by circumstance in addition to my amateurish execution.

Deciding not to cook is a perfectly metropolitan thing to do, and I perfectly respect that mentality assuming there is sufficient wealth to negotiate that self-inflicted weakness. A Rockefeller, for instance, shall retain the right to not cook at all, because their army of servants could surely perform those duties sufficiently and leave said Rockefeller to attend to more important matters. That being said, should anything happen to change the station of said Rockefeller, he or she would be in a particularly compromised position... not having the ability to prepare even the most simple of consumable nourishment.

For me, learning to cook was born out of necessity during my early adulthood as a result of being young and poor. I always packed a lunch for work and rarely ate out as per my natural tendency to save money. Eating out is vastly more expensive than cooking for yourself, and generally less healthy. One of the ways restaurants make food so delicious is by using lots of fats and salt. Butter, oil, mayo, cheese... these are a few of my favorite things. Especially at the time, the cost of eating at home was almost negligible compared to eating at restaurants. If you're any good at cooking it can be a better experience because you know exactly what you are getting and get to taste the sweet pride of doing a good job.

I remember as a fourteen yr old kid, making four dollars and fifteen cents per hour working at my dad's bike and hobby store, riding my bike to the grocery store to buy chicken thighs for thirty nine cents a pound and a twelve pack of soda for dollar ninety nine to have a BBQ party with my friends. With one hour of labor I had enough money to host a barbecue party for something like six people. Now obviously costs have changed, even the proportion of minimum wage versus food purchasing power has gotten significantly worse. However, just as back then, buying raw food products at the grocery store and preparing them at home is significantly less expensive than eating out at restaurants. If a single meal at a restaurant is $15 (getting harder to find by the day), you could feed your family of four at home for about that amount. So it's not a savings of fifteen or twenty five percent, it's like four to ten times less expensive.

Especially when feeding a family, cooking at home means more and better control over what your family is eating, all but guaranteeing a healthier diet. It also means more control over how much you spend even as it relates to home cooked meals. While spaghetti and meatballs might run up past $10 for the family meal, there are many options that are so inexpensive that the cost seems negligible.

I've got my boys convinced that ramen is a special meal. Partly because we don't eat it very often and I dance it up with some onion, cilantro, and some cabbage if we have any. The whole meal might cost less than a dollar and that's in today's economy, when before this latest trend in inflation it might have been less than 50 cents. It's not a sacrifice, it's good and the kids love it. It's easy and fast and inexpensive, just don't overdo it by eating it all the time or your kids will resent you forever.

Part of what makes me so well qualified to write a book about being frugal is that I come from a long line of frugal people on both sides of my family. Both my grandfathers were particularly thrifty, no doubt because they grew up during the great depression where frugality was not a preference but a very real necessity. My dad and uncles all inherited that trait and kept company with people that had similar values. One of my dad's best friends has got to be the cheapest person I know, perhaps to a fault. Actually, definitely to a fault. He took thriftiness to a new level. Notice I didn't call him the thriftiest person, because he is the cheapest. His thriftiness regularly went too far and ended up acting as a sort of subtle punishment his family was obligated to endure.

In his credit, he never wasted a cent and instead invested every last penny that ever came into his possession. He therefore was able to amass an extensive real-estate portfolio in coastal central California which has now matured, making him and his family extraordinarily wealthy, though you'd never know by looking at him. You see, old habits die hard and even as a millionaire you'll find him dining on a can of sardines for dinner as he has become accustomed to the simple stoicism of un-indulgent habits. His daughters will roll their eyes and go out for sushi instead, accepting that though he can easily afford to eat five star every night, spending that kind of money to eat is not in his nature and produces a foul taste to his time-tested sensibilities. For him it's a religion of sorts, that rejects the self-indulgent gluttony of our wealthy era. To each his own; but I prefer to live extraordinarily well while at the same time saving as much of my money as possible for more important endeavors.

I've been working on my cooking skills consistently since early adulthood and before. My step mom Colleen was a fabulous cook and opened my eyes to the valuable experiences produced by good food. Her policy was for my dad, my sister, and I to each cook dinner one night per week and she would prepare excellent meals the other four nights a week. Back in those days I was a one trick pony and would rarely stray from my main go to: casseroles. Tuna, green bean, or occasionally an authentic homemade macaroni and cheese or meatloaf to throw everyone off the scent of one trick ponyness. A favorite after school snack was quesadillas with flour tortillas fried in butter. That simple comb produced a browned and crispy quesadilla that rivaled any produced by a restaurant when served with sour cream and guacamole made from one of the plentiful avocados that little town was famous for.

We rarely ate at restaurants and I hardly noticed because our lives were so culinarily rich despite. Colleen would make chicken cordon bleu, wonderful pastas, roasts served with asparagus or brussel sprouts, and an ever evolving menu of equally enticing dishes that put all but the finest restaurants to shame. Brussel sprouts, by the way, are one of the most underrated vegetables and get an undeserved bad rap from forces within media that at every opportunity in sitcoms and movies insist kids don't like them, which in my experience is not true at all. We hardly ever ate at restaurants and we were not missing anything. We were eating healthier, better food, at home, for a much better value. It was not a sacrifice, it was an improvement.

My wife and I have friends that eat out or order in for almost every meal and it's sometimes comical to hear them discuss dinner plans. They'll banter about proposing Papa Johns or Panda Express or one of the many local fine dining spots, taking turns to counter the other with, "we ate that last week" or "I had that yesterday". They're getting bored with the local selection of restaurants, of which there are many and many of which are quite good. There's no adventure in their culinary experience because to them it's commonplace. There are three meals a day and they eat out or order in at least two of them. That's fourteen meals per week. With numbers like that it's not surprising they've exhausted the expansive local selection. Not to mention the money they are spending to support this habit.

If they were wealthy I would chalk it up to the Rockefeller example I cited above. The thing is that they are not. They don't even own their own home. The quantity of money they are spending just feeding themselves is more than enough to cover a generous mortgage for a wonderful home. Theoretically they could exchange eating from restaurants for a beautiful house and an investment property. Then after years of investing and flipping up their investment properties they would become wealthy to the point of being able to eat out every meal without it affecting their comfortable retirement plans. It really comes down to: do you want to look rich, or do you want to become rich.

Learning to cook for yourself is an investment that throughout your lifetime will net you quite literally millions of dollars if you correctly invest the money that you save, as witnessed by the examples I gave above. You can start small with basics that you can gradually improve over time. With each meal you cook you will improve your skills and eventually you will be able to impress your friends and family where they will prefer your food over restaurants the way I preferred Colleen's food, or more recently my wife's.

My wife and I use cooking as a way to showcase our class, distinction, and sophistication for our friends and neighbors. It's not a sacrifice we make to save money. It's a way for us to live a privileged life of enjoyment, in keeping with the French philosophy I outlined in the beginning. We're giving our kids the privilege of a refined palate that our friends are constantly impressed with. No one can believe that our young boys love vegetables and will at least try anything that is put in front of them. They are familiar with Thai food, Japanese, Italian, French cooking, Sushi, Guatemalan, and a host of other culinary disciplines because it's what we make at home.

Their culinary class and sophistication is self-evident to any who interact with them. Coupled with their well traveled cultured dispositions, they have the advantage of being admired by other children and adults alike. It's a wonderful gift to give to them and it's something money can't buy. Later on we'll talk about how planning ahead and having systems in place to make preparing healthy delicious food for your family easy and cost effective from a perspective of time.

Busy people often feel they don't have the time to prepare their own food, but from my perspective, I don't have the time to eat out as often as they do. For me cooking is a therapeutic endeavor and I can use that time to both relax and de-stress from my job while at the same time setting up the coming week for smooth and easy meal prep that makes ordering delivery seem slow and inefficient.

CASINOS: WHERE MONEY GOES TO DIE

From what I can tell, the most dangerous thing, or perhaps more accurately, the stupidest thing you can do for the 'value for life / dollar spent' thing you can do would be to spend money on things that appease your own ego.

Remember, money is effectively time. Human time. Human hours spent. Even if you make your money in a way other than trading your time for money, everyone else is trading their time for money. Wasting money is like wasting time or wasting life.

Islam has this interesting principle: you should spend your money effectively because wasting your money is a sin because it is an insult to all of the people that helped you make that money. This is not a bad way to look at it. Yes it's yours, congratulations, but don't disrespect the situation you inherited from society as to be in such a good position as to have enough money to waste. People that have enough money to waste are not exactly the target market for this book, but in a way, we're all wasting money. This book is a guide on how to get better value for the money that you have, for the things that really matter.

The biggest waste of money I can think of is gambling. I grew up in Lake Tahoe, near the border between California and Nevada. This was before Indian casinos. Across the border in Nevada, starting exactly on the border, stood tall magnificent casino buildings. Bright lights, neon signs, shiny glass that could not be seen into from the outside (except the buffet floors that taunted the hungry passersby).

A friend of mine's dad worked as a slot machine technician and taught his son an important lesson at an early age: "See those tall buildings, see those bright lights? Who do you think pays for all that? Do you think winners pay for all that? Nope, losers pay for all that." As in, the construction, the electricity, the staff, the everything, is all paid for by people losing at the games the casinos offer.

It might feel awesome to throw money around like a big shot, but you'd better actually be a big shot. If you're not a big shot, then gambling is not only a giant waste of time at best, but generally a stupid endeavor, and a life destroyer at worst. Even big shots become small frys if they have the bug bad enough.

Chris Webber, the basketball player for the Sacramento Kings, would regularly blow millions of dollars at the casinos in my town. If you haven't heard of him, I'm not surprised, apparently the dude was a loser. In my opinion, if you like the rush of taking risks you'd be better to go skydiving or boar hunting and you'd have a higher likelihood of not seriously damaging your trajectory to a better financial future.

BARTER YOUR TIME

When I was a young contractor I had a friend who was also a young contractor. In fact, he led the way, getting his C17 Glazing license, most commonly used for installing windows, before I got my "B" General Contracting license. I worked for him as a foreman managing his crews, for what was probably about a year before getting my own contracting license.

We had both worked side by side for the same General Contractor who had plans to retire and was generous enough to share some of the business intel we would need to get started on our own. When I first started working for him this was his pitch to me: "I'm retiring in the next few years and I'm happy to share what I know about how to run a successful contracting business". What an opportunity. How could I say no? It went basically as he had stated. I worked for a few years, he was generous with what he taught me, and eventually he retired.

After a few years working for Bob, I went off to India on an eleven week adventure. A slim but fit 165lb, I returned 140 lbs. At 6' 2", that's skinnier than Abraham Lincon in his backyard wrestling days. When I got back, my mentor Bob had retired. It took some time to heal and gain weight again and by the time I was healthy, and after some time of working on my own, Craig had already started his business and eventually was ready for some help. It was a natural progression. Craig had a good crew and I learned a lot managing them.

When it was time for me to go out on my own, I did. It was 2008 and I was approaching my 31st birthday.

On my way to take the contractors exam the radio announced that Lehman Brothers had filed for bankruptcy. I was tuned in enough to know that many of the people that I had worked for in the meantime were using construction loans to develop their properties. A banking crisis was surely bad news. What was I supposed to do? I took the test, passed with flying colors (I had over-studied as it turned out), and got my contractors license.

I kept in good contact with Craig and from time to time we would require each other's help, and eventually we came up with an arrangement that worked out great. Since I had confidence in his skills and he had confidence in mine, we valued each other's time equally. This might be the hard part for anyone hoping to replicate this arrangement. We would trade hours, one for one, and settle up at the end of each year. Since our exchange was more or less even, the end of the year might leave a balance of 11 or 21 or some negligible amount of outstanding hours on the part of one or the other. Since it was a relatively low balance we would just let the balance continue to ride to the next year, eventually settling up at the end of the agreement, when Craig left town. Trading hours was a way for us to leverage our skills and abilities into the abilities of others. This was a very useful play and makes for much simpler paperwork than the alternative.

THINGS

One man's trash is another man's treasure. This means, if you have the means to store and hold something until you finally find someone who values it more than you, you can make a profit, or at least keep something useful in circulation. I suppose the hard part is having the place and the space. Even if you have the space you'll probably face some kind of hell from your wife, landlord, mom, or neighbors; just for trying to keep said things from being erased into the global trash heap forever.

It's also a humanitarian endeavor. People make a big deal about saving the environment, while they order new halloween decorations from Amazon. Made in China, disposable, covered in glittery macro-plastics, shipped from Atlanta to Nashville to Tucson, to Los Angeles, to Seattle, back to Tucson, to a distribution facility in Nashville, back to Atlanta, then shipped to the final customer. Then used for one month and set out on the curb to be destroyed only 9 months from needing to be re-ordered again. The people that talk most about the environment are the ones that appear to care the least about it.

What's more wasteful? Ordering Valentine's decoration or saving a commercial meat slicer you found at the dump that probably only needs to have the connections re-made? You will need to re-make those connections (unless it's something else (in which case figure out whatever that might be)), and store and wait until the right buyer comes along. Your wife is employing an army of underaged communist child laborers to manufacture her holiday decoration while you are preserving timeless mechanical relics that are useful and have the potential to provide value to the human experience. We men deal with such unspeakable injustice on a daily basis. The horror. The horror.

For me to have any amount of righteous dignity while purveying this book, I must be honest in every respect. That means covering the details that affect the readers to the best of my knowledge.

This means I can not allow, for any of my readers, under my advice, to misconstrue my instructions to mean that it is justified to hold some item for better than 10 years... unless it is a very special or technologically important artifact or has some artistic or vintage value. In that case, you have my full endorsement to divorce, separate, sever, or completely disavow anyone who prefers empty space over respecting the natural value of something that is useful and took man-hours to make and has lasted until now. Don't hoard, unless you can get away with it, and in that case, don't hoard junk with no value ... in other words, Chinese junk ... unless it's really old.

Think of everything you have as consuming rent. Even if you are not paying rent, your space is rentable and therefore should be regarded as having some kind of value. If you pay rent on something for 10 years and don't get any value in return, that was a waste and that space should have been relegated to something more productive. Also, after 10 years, most things degrade and become less valuable. Waiting for something to become an antique is a fool's errand. There's plenty of people already doing that and you can just pick that stuff up at their estate sale after they die if you're interested in antiques.

So I guess it's really about discipline. If you acquire things that need to be repaired, make sure that you make weekly progress on repairing them. If you have things that are not useful to you, you need to make weekly progress on selling them. If you have items for sale that are not getting any interest, you need to actively seek out the right party to barter for something that is useful to you. If you can't do that, think of someone you can give them to, thus returning them to useful circulation and liberating the space of yours that they use up. Respect the intrinsic value of things and the investment the world made in time and resources to create them and try to set the universe straight by putting those things back into service, delivering value to the right person. It's good karma and your wife will reward you for it.

You know how stores have end of season sales to blow out their remaining inventory at bargain prices to make room for the new years products? They do this because they pay rent and the stuff they don't sell takes up the room that a newer, more saleable product could inhabit. Also because the stuff that's left apparently doesn't sell as well as the stuff that sold. As time goes on it will become less saleable and eventually reflect poorly on their establishment as a whole. If they were to keep that old stuff, their store will eventually become known as the store that sells old stuff nobody wants. That's not a very attractive image, is it?

When your garage starts to get crowded, remember this principle and have your own blow-out sale as a means to prevent yourself from becoming that old curmudgeon that prefers the value of dusty old junk over things that are useful and can be put to more productive endeavors.

Buying at garage sales is a great way to benefit from the materialism of others. You'll find great stuff, sometimes better than their modern and available counterparts, for pennies on the dollar. You might find a blender that has worked flawlessly for fifteen years, that will work for fifteen more before eventually needing to be serviced and then put back into action for another thirty years. This is something modern blenders are not capable of thanks to an engineering principle called engineered obsolescence. Products from the era before scumbag business people decided to intentionally make their products worse to keep you in a constant cycle of spending to buy things you already have because the piece of crap broke because it was designed to.

I speak of blenders with experience. My mom had an Osterizer blender. It was a wedding gift from the ancient past I can't even begin to guess when, as she was at this point divorced from my dad for at least 10 years. It worked fine, as it had done so its entire faithful service life which was apparently not over yet. Despite its loyal fidelity, my mom decided to get rid of it because she didn't like the color. She replaced it with a candy-apple red blender that looked like a quality model. It had a glass pitcher, similar controls, and appeared to be very much the same thing except red. Not a day past one year later, the damn thing stopped working. Every year since my mom has bought a new blender, thus fulfilling the prophecy of those wicked engineered obsolescence people and filling the world with useless junk and binding us all in the invisible chains of materialist servitude.

The previous story perfectly illustrates the wickedness of materialism and wonderful salvation that is garage sales. The pitfall with garage sales is that you will end up buying things you don't need and thus falling into your own materialist hole where instead of wasting money (you ARE actually wasting money, just not as much as if you were obsessively buying new stuff with the same vigor), you're wasting space, and wasting the value of those objects by keeping them out of useful circulation: pent up in your garage gathering dust like a soviet dissident in the depths of a Siberian gulag. Utilize garage sales and thrift shops to find things of value to yourself and your friends, but use a disciplined approach.

Realize the danger exists to buy something just because it's a really good bargain, or just because you respect the value or historical significance of the object.

Remember to only buy with a purpose. If you buy something to then later sell, strategically assess the process to do that. Does it need to be cleaned, repaired, listed on an online marketplace, packaged and delivered? Do you have the time to do that and will you make enough to justify spending the time to do that? If you work a full time job the answer to the last question is probably no as you are better to spend your free time enjoying the company of your family.

Is this a business or a hobby? If you are not buying for a business then you need to be particularly disciplined and not let the allure of an incredible deal cloud your judgment. Use techniques to stay on the path. Call your sponsor, or better yet, take a picture of the item and text it to a friend that might be able to use it. If you can't think of anyone to pass that deal on to, then forget about it. It means you have no way to bring that wonderful object into productive circulation and the seller is in a better position to set the universe straight than you are. Then let it go. Literally forget about it, as to not let it muddy your thoughts, dwelling on it as a missed opportunity. It's not a missed opportunity, it's an opportunity to waste space, waste the object's intrinsic value and productive potential, and piss off your wife and or landlord and neighbors. Take solace that you've already assessed the opportunistic value of the purchase and deemed it a poor fit. Now move on with life.

The QuickPass

If you can trust yourself with Garage Sailing, we need to talk about the "Quick Pass".

As you know, I have a background in construction. Remodels to be specific. This means lots of interior work that is under scrutiny of sometimes very careful eyes. Over the years I've had the distinct pleasure of educating many helpers and employees about the intricacies of the multitude of processes that comprise an interior and or exterior remodel. One principle is the "quickpass".

A quick pass is a process that can be used in a number of scenarios and basically translates to "get only the lowest lying fruit". From drywall to painting to putty to cleanup, a quickpass means, do this job as though your pants are on fire. For thrift stores, garage sales, and discount markets, a quickpass means peruse the inventory as though you need to use the bathroom really badly. As in number two. As in, don't waste a second to think too much about anything, don't indulge any silly fantasies, and only take a second look if something both fills an existing need you have and screams out that it's a fantastic deal.

It's first of all a psychological device to prevent your idle mind from imagining any ridiculous scenarios where you invent a different version of yourself that has the time, abilities, and inclination to repair, rebuild, or resell any of the many interesting and potentially repairable, rebuildable, and resellable items you are likely to find during a walkthrough of a thrift store or garage sale.

Ideally, you would be in too much of a hurry for your imagination to get any wise ideas so remember to keep your feet moving and your eyeballs scanning. Technically, your eyeballs should be slightly behind your feet. It's better to miss a few things that go slow enough for your imagination to catch up and ruin the whole thing with stupid and unrealistic ideas about how you will make use of something that will actually only serve as a dust collector in a part of your garage better utilized as free space to repair the things in your life that you actually need and use. If you were picking apples, you'd only be picking the ones that had already fallen on the ground.

The Gift of Thrift

You'll know you have achieved mastery of the quickpass when you can walk into and out of a thrift store in less than three minutes without buying anything, and, here's the kicker: and not giving a second thought to any of the things you left behind. If it doesn't happen on your first time, don't worry, that's normal. It takes practice and experience to eventually become numb to nostalgia and thrill of the deal that plague beginners as they slowly stroll the aisles with open mouths and glazed eyes entertaining their most ridiculous imaginations like a bunch of soft bellied amateurs looking to nibble bait off the hooks of seasoned veteran fisherman. They are playing with fire and have yet to learn their lesson. They're two garage sales of their own away from learning that they will not live as long as their ambitions insist they will.

Owning the quickpass means briskly walking with the same smug disinterest you would show if you were walking past a television showing a mediocre movie you had regretfully already seen against your will more than once. If the inventory were a person you would not make eye-contact as to avoid any possible emotional connection that might elicit an irrational response. Cold as ice, no eye-contact, no imagination, no optimism, no emotion. A quickpass is reconnaissance only mode. If something snags your attention, take it back to intel and they can make the decision. This means when you are of sound mind you can evaluate the deal when it is not staring you in the face, seducing your weakest tendencies, like sunkist mediterranean sirens serenading lovesick sailors after a month on the lonely seas.

Let me give you an example:

I was doing a quickpass at the local thrift store in Tahoe as I had a few minutes before I had to be somewhere. I took my normal route. On my way in I noticed the "30% off with purchase of $20 or more" sign and continued on my rounds. Second turn I spotted a guitar, and as a musician I took note. Nothing special from what I could tell, broken strings, dusty, old. The price tag seemed odd: $135, gosh, they seemed pretty proud of the old thing. I finished up my rounds and came back to the dusty old relic. What would give them the impression that a dusty old unplayable guitar would be worth $135? Intrigue was beginning to set in. I gave it a closer look. The neck was straight, had no visible damage except a couple of dings, the strings were mostly broken or missing and it couldn't be played in situ, but I was able to assess that it was playable, should new strings be installed.

With a quick pass of the cuff to brush off some of the ancient dust, like a genie from a lamp, it revealed its majesty. This was not just any guitar, this guitar was special. I pulled out my phone and did a quick internet search. Bingo, people were asking $800+ for the same model. Remember, it was 30% off day so I got it for just more than a hundred bucks, so that plus a pair of strings and a thorough wipedown I had scored what has now become my favorite guitar, beating out five other guitars that all cost me multiples more except the $60 one I got in Tijuana when I was 14.

The quickpass works at garage sales but since garage sales are generally one day affairs, if you find something, you have to decide quickly because the deals have legs and will walk off if you so much as go to your car to think about it. It's perfect for thrift stores and discount grocery stores where you can, over time, become familiar with inventory and prices and thus gain the uncanny ability of spotting the outrageous deals instantly without hardly any effort at all. When you spot a deal you can snag it, and if you've done it right, even your wife can't blame you for it.

Just yesterday I did a quickpass at our local Grocery Outlet. For any readers familiar with the discount grocery chain, I've been told I look like one of their puppet mascots,

Been Savin. Despite our obvious likeness, the namesake element has me suspicious to say the least.

Once, my roommate said to a friend of ours that was visiting for the day, "Doesn't Ben look like Ben Savin?" pointing to a Grocery Outlet circular in what was basically a soft insult directed at yours truly. My visiting friend, bless his heart, not being singled out for his astuteness in that moment responded, "no, or, I mean, maybe if he was a puppet." Even though I was stung by the insult originally intended by my roommate, I couldn't help but erupt into laughter alongside my roommate as my guest tilted his head to help comprehend what it was we had found so funny. Yes, Been Savin only looks like me if I were a puppet, to whom it may concern.

So, at yesterday's quick pass through Grocery Outlet (I stopped because I needed to burn some time because the boys were sleeping in their carseats in back and I couldn't shut off the engine because they would wake and crankeyness would ensue), I exercised a 9/10 quick pass that numbers wise was a top ten, but all in all is testament to my mastery of my very own Grocery Outlet Quick Pass System (GOQPS). No eye-contact, no emotion, just as I mentioned before. I walked the aisles in the regular fashion, fast and as cold as ice. I was disappointed that the pickles I wanted at the great price in the jar I wanted were not there but I didn't stop to lament or mourn, I pressed on, like any good bargain shopper would do. I passed one of the bigger tags I've trained my eyes to pick out: 4 / 97 cents. That's intriguing.

It was for a 50 oz can of Campbell's "low sodium tomato soup". The soup was an obvious deal and I was also interested in the can for its rocket-stove possibilities (spoiler alert, the 50 oz can is probably only suitable for a mini rocket-stove and not exactly ideal for even that). Four of them for 97 cents, USD. I only bought 2 of them because I was concerned my wife might make fun of me, making the quickpass a 9/10 instead of a 10/10. In hindsight I would have been better to have bought 8, at the staggering price of just under two dollars. US dollars, if you can believe that, and it's a perfectly wonderful soup, especially if served with a grilled cheese sandwich.

DISCOUNT MARKETS

Ok, so here's the thing with Grocery Outlet: The products in that store are generally there for a reason. Why would Campbell's give their products away for so cheap, it's obviously not because they were feeling generous. When I read the label I immediately had a pretty good idea what was wrong. Low Sodium. This either caused it to not taste good (which is what happens when I don't put enough salt in the food I cook), or caused it to not sell well, or in this case: both. Either situation could cause Campbell's to offload the whole lot for pennies to Grocery Outlet. As it turned out, it was the salt, or lack of it. This is something I have a solution for.

My years of culinary expertise had prepared me for this very moment. On my own, without so much as a google search I was able to come up with an impromptu solution for this situation. I added about two tablespoons of salt and it tastes just like the original Campbell's tomato soup we have all come to love over the years. Go figure. Now you can see how I could have scored 10/10 simply by spending another $1.50 to buy six more to last us through the end of the year. But let's not get too cheap and burn the kids out on tomato soup forever.

At Grocery Outlet, something is always wrong. It doesn't mean the products are bad, but it does mean that something is wrong. It's your job as a bargain shopper to figure out what that is. If you're too busy, or important, or self righteous; Whole Foods is happy to do your thinking for you at a generous premium.

Grocery Outlet is a discount 'grocery outlet', meaning that in addition to the basic staples that they acquired through normal means, they have food products that suffer from one or more issues that affect their saleability. Most common is probably spicy. Since spicy is probably hard to gauge when dealing with fresh chilies, some recipes go wrong at the factory and end up way spicier than originally intended.

What does a manufacturer do when they have 30k units of jalapeno hummus that is way spicier than intended? They sell it to Grocery Outlet and other discount grocery vendors at pennies on the dollar in order to recoup their packaging and materials costs and hopefully a bit more if they are lucky. If you like spicy, you are in luck. If it's super cheap and is in some way labeled as spicy, it's probably way spicier that it is labeled. That brings me to the next reason you'll see products for crazy low prices.

Labeling Errors are the best deals at discount grocery chains like Grocery Outlet because it means there is literally nothing wrong with the product, just that it was labeled incorrectly and therefore is not fit to be sold in premium grocery markets. Sometimes there will be a printed sticker placed above the printed information on the package and other times it will be like the example above, where the package says it's mildly spicy when in reality it's take the top of your head off spicy.

Sometimes it will be something benign and silly, that you wouldn't have even noticed even if someone had told you, like the nutritional information table on the back says it contains 5 mg of niacin when in reality it only contains 3 mg. Other times it might be more significant, like it was labeled as organic, and had been relabeled as "Not Organic", which obviously would be a poor seller in premium markets. Best is when it's a spelling error or some dumb formatting problem with the label. Same product, stupid label, half price… oh yeah, I'll take that one all day long.

Expiration dates are another reason products end up at Grocery Outlet. Some people go through their pantries and throw out anything that's even close to its expiration date. If you yourself do this, can you do me a favor and at least donate it to a food bank or someone who might be able to make use of it, because in all likelihood it's fine, and your overprecation is wasting food that more hungry people than yourself could be eating. Would you imagine that the manufacturer knows exactly when a can of green beans will go bad?

"Sir, on exactly February 11, 2024 this can of beans will expire." says Ensign Forthright.

"God help those who open it on February 12" Admiral Greenbean replies.

"God help them indeed, sir" Ensign Forthright solemnly replies.

This is not how it goes down. Expiration dates are the best assessment of how long the packaging will last, and always with a comfortable margin as to avoid the terrible liability involved in getting it wrong.

Imagine you were in a post-apocalyptic situation where you were literally starving to death. Your left foot had already rotted off as a result of a stubbed toe, and thank goodness for some amoxicillin you looted from an abandoned pharmacy, you did not die from infection. Your youngest had already died from consumption and your two still living were hungry and not looking particularly healthy. You have a can of chili but it's five years expired. The can shows no signs of damage, no dents or swelling. When opened the contents look and smell fine. Will you try your luck to kill another rabbit with the few remaining rounds of ammunition you have left, or will you give them the expired chili? I'm not trying to bum you out, I'm just saying that a quick reality check makes the obvious answer an astounding yes. Open the damn chili and give thanks for what you still have.

At discount markets like Grocery Outlet there might be products that are approaching their expiration date, in which case, pay attention to that and don't put those in your pantry for long term storage. Eat them soon, or not too long after expiration, but don't save them for an apocalypse that may never come. Grocery Outlet won't sell food that's past expiration, and I'll never forgive them for that.

Just the other day I went back to Grocery Outlet because they had these wonderful little packets of salami sticks for 77 cents. Lucky me, they still had them, and as this was a quick pass before work I was keeping a brisk pace. I thought to myself, "Those Cheddar cheese sticks they had ten for one dollar would serve as a nice accompaniment to these delicious salamis". Moving at a brisk pace, cold as ice, with no emotion or attachment to outcome I went to the place where the cheese sticks should be. Weird, there were none. A quick glance around and I found a beautiful young latin woman stocking the cheese section and a rolling rack with boxes nearby. On the rolling rack I saw a box with jumbo bags that probably held something like two hundred cheese sticks each. I asked the girl where the cheese sticks were, knowing full well that they were on the rolling cart, expecting her to say something like,

"Oh, let me get you some, I haven't unpacked them yet".

Instead, to my horror, she said, "I'm sorry, those are expired, we can't sell them"

I said, "Can you give them to me?"

"No, we can't do that either." She shamefully muttered, aware of the absurdity as the words left her mouth.

I was this close to asking her which dumpster she was planning on throwing them into and if she could just meet me out back and hand me the box before it touches the inside of that regrettably sinful dumpster that wastefully consumes more calories per day than a third term African Elephant on a midsummer Saharan evening. What in God's name would cause people to become so wasteful?

Live Better but Cheaper

Look, I like saving money, but dumpster diving is something I will not do. Not only because it would ruin the saleability of this book. If word got out that yours truly was going into trash cans to save money, the whole gig would be up.

Listen, if this were an apocalyptic scenario, it's like the cockroach example I made in the beginning. Never say never. But I thank God that I have never been in a position to need to eat a cockroach, or to go into a dumpster to get food. As a reader, I don't think you'd need a book to tell you how to do that.

Truthfully, it's probably a cornucopia of wonderful stuff, if you don't mind getting dirty to get it. But then again, the point of the book is not to humiliate yourself by eating the scraps of other people because your life decisions have left you with no other choices but to accept your place among the lowest rungs of human dignity. This book is about elevating your sophistication and class by saving money where you can so that you can invest into things that will eventually lead you to real wealth. Instead of pretending that you are wealthy now, or giving up on the idea of wealth entirely and jumping into the dumpster to get those excellent and definitely still-good cheese sticks.

Look how my pretentious self image kept me from enjoying months of free cheese. Just because I grew up privileged, was taught manners and class by my mother who read Emily Post and attended finishing school in North Carolina before shipping off to Art College in Switzerland to study theater and art. My dad, of more humble beginnings, grew up on the humble shores of Palos Verdes, California, overlooking the Los Angeles valley. I myself was so disadvantaged as to have no live-in maid, no gardener, and my poor father was tasked with managing the pool, sauna, and hot-tub by himself. It's a wonder that I survived at all. Oh, for shame.

I wasn't about to dive into any dumpsters for cheese sticks, as I'm sure my readers would likewise not pay extra for advice that leads them into that program. But, do throw me a bone here: I was incensed that my beloved Grocery Outlet would be so brazen as to waste such a valuable and shelf-stable resource as cheese. I personally have cheese that's more than 2 years old. That's the whole thing with cheese!! They can't even put it out to market until it's like 6 months old. It seems a little petty to me to say that after 6 months they put it to market, but at exactly eight and a half months it must be thrown in a dumpster.

I say let it ride. If it goes bad, then don't eat it. Let's say the packaging fails and somehow the cheese goes bad. At that point it would be obvious. The package would be swollen, the cheese would be covered in mold. Nothing dangerous could happen with a giant bag of cheese sticks. Worst case scenario is some of them won't be edible. Part of me thinks that in cold storage, they could be awesome in like five years or so. Maybe it's just me.

I haven't mentioned it specifically but my number one mentor for frugality in this world (I've had many), is my dad. My dad's brand is a bit more refined, with elements of class and sophistication that I appreciate, and combined with my mom's finishing education, I'm an amalgamation of the two of them: perhaps not as frugal as my dad, whom is not nearly as classy as my mom, but also no slouch either;

leaving me to be frugal by nature and classy by nurture. I won't be diving into any dumpster if that's what you're asking, but my father's part of me kind of wishes I did.

FRUGALITY CAN MAKE YOU RICH

I don't want to gross you guys out, but remember the real-estate millionaire from earlier that sometimes prefers to eat sardines for dinner over sushi? Yeah him. So listen: He's been known to eat Campbell's condensed soups out of the can, cold. You have to go back and remember that he is a Stoic and prefers not to indulge in earthly delights. One time, when I was a young man, perhaps 14 or so, he made a demonstration of sorts I would never forget. We were in the kitchen and I can't remember the particulars of the situation but there was a moldy piece of cheese in the fridge that was wrapped in plastic wrap.

Plastic wrap is super efficient both for money and for plastic consumption. Zip-loc's are generally unnecessary except for when they are the perfect tool for the job, but we can talk about that later. So, moldy cheese, wrapped in plastic wrap. I assumed he was trying to teach me a valuable lesson about how and why you don't throw away cheese just because it's got a bit of mold on it. For the record, it didn't have just a bit of mold on it. It was completely covered in mold. He took it out of the plastic wrap and cut one of the moldy ends off. Again, I thought he was making a lesson of how to save cheese that has become moldy. No. He took the moldy piece that he had cut off and placed it in his mouth. He chewed it up and swallowed it. In short: he ate it.

He did not die, or even get sick for that matter. In fact the mold might have even had some antibiotic properties as antibiotics are derived from different molds. But I'm sure it didn't taste good. Mold smells and tastes like dirt, because dirt is full of mold and mold spores. It's certainly disgusting to have a mouth full of what tastes like dirt, even more disgusting to acknowledge that it's actually a piece of moldy cheese, but it makes for an impressionable demonstration. It demonstrates two things: first: that cheese mold is not dangerous, it just tastes bad; and second: that the person making the demonstration has a high tolerance for discomfort, and that, besides being disgusting, is an admirable trait.

I can only assume that he did not enjoy it, but that was his way. Generally speaking, I don't think this man enjoyed food at all. Food for him was a vehicle. You need it to go from place to place, but it's not necessary to enjoy it. You can simply consume it in its various forms, and as long as it goes down your throat and into your stomach, then it performs its duty. The part where it has to go past your tongue, in your mouth, before it can get into your throat down to your stomach, where it actually begins to do something useful, and then can be used to locomote your body around, is the part where you have the opportunity to enjoy the process.

To him, this was optional and something about the indulgent nature of it rubbed him the wrong way. In his defense, to him, eating was like going to a gas station. Do you crave the gas you put in your car? Do you get the high octane gas and savor it as your car consumes it? Probably not. That's kind of like Huntly. He prefers not to look at food that way. While I might think he's missing out on a great pleasure in life, he's there to remind me that some people vastly overrate it to their detriment and it's something you can definitely live without.

My argument goes something like: "Yes, you can live without the enjoyment of eating great food, but why would you want to?"

It sounds like my French uncle Jean Philip made an important impression on me, doesn't it? I'm glad he did, because it balances out some of the other influences I've had growing up and shed light on an interesting philosophy that I've come to incorporate into my life and family's values.

I'm also glad to have been influenced by Huntly throughout my life while at the same time glad he wasn't my father, and that my father had a well balanced approach to food and the enjoyment of it. Huntly's girls were my age and eventually grew up to be wonderfully well balanced women (no doubt with the help of their mom who was a beautiful and extraordinarily classy woman). I'm sure they appreciate their childhood and clearly love and respect their father, but that being said, I bet they never want to see top-ramen ever again.

Recently Huntly's eldest daughter Alesha was visiting us in Guatemala and somehow in a conversation about seafood the subject of mussels came up. At the mere mention of the word mussels Alesha visibly winced. This caught my attention because she is not a picky eater. "What? You don't like mussels?" I inquired. She went on to tell a story about how her dad took her and her younger sister to the beach with a five gallon bucket to crawl along the rocks of the California coast gathering mussels. The girls had a wonderful time and were prolific mussel gatherers. That night they feasted on the rewards of their labors and gorged themselves on delicious fresh mussels. By about day three they began to regret gathering so many, and by about day six, they never wanted to see another mussel again as long as they lived. On subsequent trips to gather mussels, mysteriously the girls were less successful at gathering them. Go figure.

I mentioned top-ramen earlier and I suppose that could do with some explanation. When I was a child our family would make the five or so hour drive from Lake Tahoe down to Santa Cruz to visit Huntly's family. Alesha was almost exactly my age and Natasha was slightly younger and the three of us were like peanut butter and jelly. My sister was four years older than Alesha and I and was very responsible for her age and thus charged with looking after us youngsters and keeping order amongst the children. Over the years they would come and visit us in

Tahoe and we had gone to visit them with some regularity so I noticed a pattern in the hindsight of all the years. After our long drive we would usually arrive in the late afternoon and after some time to get settled and catch up with the girls, dinner would be served. Dinner almost every time we visited was top-ramen. There were four in our family and four in theirs, so I'd have to assume we were looking at something like six packets of ramen. This was no ordinary ramen either. It had onion, cabbage, maybe even some grated carrot or some frozen peas thrown in.

  You could tell when Huntly served it he was brimming with self satisfaction, and not just that he had produced a particularly tasty ramen, but mostly that he was satisfied he had delivered it with such incredible value. Six packets, half an onion, a piece of cabbage, half a carrot, and a handful of frozen peas. It was probably back in those days less than a dollar for all of us to eat. Had we gone out to dinner we would have certainly spent upwards of a hundred dollars. That wasn't necessary and in his eyes would have been a terrible waste, in addition to an unsound investment. It wasn't that he didn't have money, it's that he was putting their money to work and wanted to put as much as he possibly could to work, thus not wasting it on day to day necessities that he could get for less, even if there was a noticeable quality difference.

Now, as a four year old there is nothing remarkable about eating ramen for dinner either way. Ramen is good, and this ramen was particularly good because it had some extra goodies that fleshed it out a bit more. It tasted good and surely provided us with the nourishment we all needed to enjoy ourselves in the beautiful California coast during our stay there. It wasn't until I was about seven or eight that I began to recognize that this was the meal that we were always served when we arrived at their home. Which is fine, I love ramen, especially the way it was prepared.

But it did dawn on me that the girls probably ate much more of it than my sister and I did, and I bet you that the trend continued until the girls were off to college. I would imagine at that point, the last ramen diner served while the girls were still at the family house was probably the last batch of ramen either of the girls ever ate. I could be wrong, but I bet by then they had reached their fill and were probably ready to move on to other culinary pursuits.

So I guess the lesson with Huntly is that it's possible to overdo it. You can't argue with his results: he turned his wife's teacher's salary and his sweat equity into a real-estate empire that will provide well for generations to come. At some point, inheritance factored into that as well but the family was already on its way to real wealth and would have been perfectly comfortable even without.

Regardless, we will use him as an extreme example at the far end of the spectrum to show that it is possible to go too far, like maybe with the cheese I was talking about before. At the same time, when you see the results of his extreme thriftiness, look at what he was able to get for it. Both are fine lessons and should be considered when designing your own personal brand of frugality. My personal brand is somewhere in between my French uncle Jean Philip who might drive for hours to obtain the correct cheese for a particular meal, and Huntly, who will eat condensed Campbell's soup cold, directly out of the can to save a buck.

SOUP SYSTEM

So I like to live well, but I like to do it within my means while staying on track with my investment goals. Soups are a way I can do this. Besides being a particularly sensible thing to eat, they are easy to make, store well, and can be reheated and served quickly; and that works for busy people who are constantly on the go.

The gist of it is this: On Sundays I deprogram from the stress of work by making soup. Call it soup therapy. I chop up a bunch of stuff and mindlessly throw it into a pot (remember I've been doing this for years so for me it's pretty much on autopilot), and let it cook. At the end I'll taste and make any final adjustments and we'll have soup for dinner. I'll let the soup cool a bit and before bed I'll use a large mug to fill quart mason jars, leaving enough headspace to allow me to freeze them. If it's winter I'll take them outside and put them in the snow so they won't heat up the freezer so much when I put them in. I'll usually leave one or two in the fridge so we can eat it again at some point in the coming week, and I'll usually take one or two previous soups out of the freezer while I'm there to put them in the fridge so we'll have some variety for the week ahead.

It has to be mason jars and here's why. A tupperware often leaks, but more importantly, needs a ladle to be unloaded. Jars work perfectly for this system and here's why. When it's time to eat you can microwave the whole jar, or just give it a shake and pour it out into a bowl or mug the desired amount and microwave that. No ladle, no mess. Mason jars can be frozen, only if you've left enough headspace at the top to allow for ice expansion. Pickle jars work great too, but can't be frozen, so I utilize those for the soup I put in the refrigerator for the next day or coming week, or for soups I'm giving away. I'll often ask neighbors and friends to save me their 16oz or larger jars and then I can give away soups and not be bitter about not getting my jar back. I have a 32 quart pot I love dearly, and this allows me to make soups at scale and be generous with them, racking up karma and favors by constantly giving away my soups. It also means that for me to keep up with my soup program for my own needs, I really only need to make soup about once per month. If you're just starting out, you'll want to do it on a smaller scale. Your soups have to be pretty awesome for people to eat thirty two quarts of them, and in the beginning, they won't be. In the beginning, mine wern't

The whole idea of this program is convenience and variety. It's convenient because it takes three minutes to microwave a jar and pour it into a thermos for lunch or come home and pour yourself a bowl and you're eating in a couple of minutes. You have to freeze so that you can build an inventory that offers selection. At any given time, my freezer might have: Chicken soup, Megastroni(minestrone doesn't have Italian sausage), Split pea, Black bean, Cauliflower Cream, Broccoli Cheddar, Potato Leek, Tomato Bisque, Tom Ka, Barley Beef, and a rotating supply that constantly changes enough to keep everyone interested while still looking forward to the old favorites.

Remember how I was saying saving money is often about planning and preparation? It's true. When I find myself overspending, it's usually because I didn't pack a lunch for work or the kids are hungry and cranky and my wife is beginning to show signs of being hungry and we stop somewhere to eat to avoid some catastrophic meltdown. When this happens the restaurant check will often be upwards of fifty dollars, and nowadays it's often closer to a hundred. If I had just packed sandwiches beforehand, that eighty five dollars would still be available to be invested or even just spent on something more fun that eating a mediocre restaurant that we happened upon because we were on the road and the kids got hungry.

Good planning means observing life's predictable outcomes and preparing accordingly. Kids get hungry. This is a thing. To neglect this obvious fact and make no corresponding preparation, you are effectively preparing to be overcome with a predictably unpredictable in situ solution that is highly likely to come with a large price tag. If you fail to plan, you plan to fail.

My wife and I will often take the kids on spontaneous long drives so they can nap while we explore. The spontaneity of this practice makes it difficult to plan for, but because we know we do this we are predictably unpredictable. This means we can plan on our unpredictability. This means we should have a permanent stash of food and snacks whenever we are in the car with the boys. If we fail to do this, eventually we will either be dealing with cranky kids, or expensive trips to restaurants. So, to reiterate, planning is key to saving money, or at least wasting less of it.

My soup routine is critical to keeping things running smoothly because always having soup on hand means we always have an easy and fast way to supplement a dinner or enjoy a light lunch with hardly any time or effort in the moment. Always having different kinds of soups available is key to not becoming bored with one soup, which jeopardizes the whole mission. First, we should talk a little bit about soup theory.

SOUP THEORY

First, even a really good soup will only be enjoyed for a maximum of two days, so don't even think of making a big pot and leaving it in the fridge for the week. Food that is no longer exciting becomes drudgery after the first couple of experiences, even if it is really good. Staying enthusiastic about soup is a critical psychological element that can not be ignored. Remember, people lie about home cooked food all the time to protect the cooks feelings. What your guests say has nothing to do with the truth whatsoever. Watch what people do instead. If they scarf it all down and ask for seconds, that means that it was good and they liked it. All other complements or signals should be disregarded and ignored unless they are specific enough to take action on, like "this could use more spice" or "it tastes watery". Feedback like this stings, but it's gold. You'll start inviting blunt or even rude people to dinner just to get real feedback on your soups, an invaluable technique. Children are also often candid critics, and it's easier to take their honesty than it is with adults.

Next, they are soups, not stews. Stews are thicker, and also delicious, but if you set out to make a soup, it should have the consistency of a soup, not thick like a stew. You don't need very much to make a soup, that was kind of the point originally. Remember, for much of human history, at least for certain times in the year (particularly winter), people didn't have very much to eat. Hence, soups. Soups are a way to stretch out food and make a little food go a long way. It's what makes them such a sensible food and perfect for anyone looking to go on an easy diet. Simply have soup for lunch instead of soup and a sandwich. Or go with soup and a salad, forgoing the sandwich or main course and you're in pretty good territory for losing weight, or at least not gaining any more. You'll feel full because, indeed, you did eat a lot, but what you ate doesn't have very much nutritional value. Remember, for most of human history people were starving most of the time (that's why you gain weight so easily), soups were a way to make starving not feel so bad.

Soups grow. Fixing a soup that has become a stew means adding more water or stock. This could end up making it huge. Especially when you are starting out, no one is going to want to eat your soup more than twice in the same week. Storing soups is critical and part of the system that will give you the variety to stay enthusiastic, but you're going to run out of room if you store five gallons of the same soup. Even if you think it tastes really good, you're probably just proud of yourself and tasting your own pride instead. Everyone else will find it bland and boring, but the first time they have it they will forgive you because the main course is on its way. Start by trying to make only enough for the meal, and you will inevitably have enough left over to put some in the fridge for tomorrow's lunch. If there's more than that, trust me it will go to waste. Wait until you've got a couple of good ones before you make big batches to save for later.

All soups require onion. Onion is such an important part of soups that it's the only ingredient that has its own soup: French Onion. This is not 100% true, but for the beginner's perspective you should treat it like it is until you level up a few times.

Do not shop for soups. Unless of course you are out of onion. Soups are a way to prevent wasting food when it is time to clean out your fridge. When you're good, you'll be able to clean out your fridge and find the things that are about at the end of their lifespan and make a delicious soup or stew from that. You do not need fresh ingredients to make soup. Save the crisp celery, firm tomatoes, and white mushrooms for your salads. When the celery gets flexible, the tomatoes get squishy, and the mushrooms start to have brown spots; it's time to make a soup. This is another thing that ends up saving you money. Instead of throwing a bunch of food in the trash each week like you normally do, you'll be making a bunch of soups instead. If you're making it from ingredients that you were going to throw away, it's basically free soup. And don't act like that's gross, it's not. That celery is still edible, it's just not particularly appetizing for a salad. It works fine for a soup, in which it will soften up anyway.

LEVEL UP TO GOURMET

Human nature is such that in our abundant society, we have enough wealth that we are not forced to eat anything. Because you always have choices, you will generally choose the best of available options, thus leaving the second, third, and worse options to get even older than they were when you rejected them, eventually throwing them in the trash. When you are looking through your fridge for something to make or eat, the things you pass up have a higher and higher likelihood of never being eaten the more times you pass them up. If the celery is too soft to put into a salad, it's not going to look any better tomorrow. You have to have an outlet for the food in your fridge that is starting to go bad. Once it starts looking unattractive, you will ignore it until eventually reality forces you to acknowledge that it is no longer edible. Make soups based on what needs to be used. This will also make you a less wasteful person.

Rich stocks are made from bones, not bullion. Yes in the beginning it might be necessary to cheat a little bit, but if you're going to give this a try, you should go all the way and try to make a real soup, the way it's really done. Not to brag, but I haven't used bullion as a soup base for years. I don't even buy salad dressing. I make my own sauces and dressings not just because they are cheaper, but it's how I avoid all the preservatives products like those need to stay good after getting mixed together. The other reason is because it's easy. I can usually whip up a sauce while my wife prepares the salad out of just a few ingredients, usually to rave reviews. Most people have a refrigerator door shelf full of dressings and sauces, all full of preservatives, and when they finally get around to checking the expiration dates on them they end up throwing most of them away. That is so wasteful. I digress, back to soup stocks.

Recently there's been a new trend surrounding bone broths. I found this kind of funny because that is what a broth is, made from bones. Everything else is just fake broth. Vegetable broths do exist but let's not get too technical for the purposes of this guide. If you're vegetarian, you have my condolences and I encourage you to find some non boring soups to simplify your mealtimes, and I wish you luck with the enthusiasm element of the soup life. For everyone else, I encourage you to use real bones to make your stocks.

Many people have no idea that soup stocks are made from bones. You take bones and you boil them. It's best if you can break the bone open to reveal the marrow, as the marrow is particularly rich, nutritious, and delicious. Or use bones from the butcher that have been sawed with a bandsaw to reveal the red interior of the bones. Spine bones or ankles or anything with lots of connective tissue tend to work particularly well. You can tell your stock is a good one because when you put it in the fridge and it cools down, it turns into jelly like jello. The better and richer it is, the thicker the consistency of the jello. This is the magic part that makes people love your soup, real stock. It's nourishing and rich and delicious, and if you served a clear broth soup made from just from stock and salted correctly, people would probably love it. Now you can experiment with adding herbs, vegetables, meats, noodles, leafy greens, etc; little by little so as to not do anything offensive that might ruin the original simplicity that was so well received.

Normally bones are something that end up as a byproduct of something else you are making, and are in that case effectively free. Once you begin to appreciate a rich base for your soups you'll find yourself buying cuts of meat that have bones that you can use for stock, and even indulge in actually buying just bones from the butcher specifically to make a stock. One thing you can do is to make a stock and then reduce it down and use some of it for the soup you are making, and put the rest in a jar in the fridge for later. When cooled it should be the consistency of a stiff jello. You could use it for other soups, or you could use it to make a sauce.

Let's say you've got some nice steaks or some pork chops or some kind of meat to be served as a main course. It's a pet peeve of mine to be served a piece of nice meat without a sauce, or worse, meat that's not properly salted. If you used a frying pan to cook your steak or chop, your pan should have greasy burnt residue stuck to it where the meat was. After you remove the meat to rest, put the pan back over the fire and splash some wine into it to deglaze that residue and put it back into the solution of the wine. Then scoop out a couple of spoonfuls of your jellied stock and drop it into the bubbling wine and watch it melt into the mixture. A little butter wouldn't hurt anything at this point and would give your sauce a nice rich body, but adding cream would do the same thing. You could use whole milk if you thought it was rich enough already. You'll need to add some salt and pepper at some point, and you could also add a dusting of flour to create a rich rue with a gravy-like texture. You could also use cornstarch to thicken up your sauce, but remember to mix it with a cold liquid like water or wine first before adding it to the pan or it will make little lumps instead of thickening your sauce evenly. Some thinly sliced mushrooms or diced green onions could be a nice addition if you have some lying around. That sauce shouldn't take but a minute to make, respects the investment you made in the meat you bought, and raises the bar on the meal you've just made. The devil is in the details, and by details, I mean sauce.

The main thing about cooking to remember is that it's not an exact science. I never measure anything and instead just start tossing stuff in incrementally and taste often. Soups are particularly forgiving because if you put too much salt, then you add more water. Start with one onion, one piece of garlic, one carrot, and one stick of celery (adding to your stock and protein of course). If it doesn't look like there is enough celery, then add another piece. Same thing with the spices, just remember to keep it simple. Don't add ten different spices. Limit it to like three or four until you begin to get more confident. Start with bayleaf, a sprig of rosemary, black pepper, and just salt. Soups get messed up because of too much complexity. Remember the holy grail of soups, French Onion. Simple is better. Don't confuse the tongue with twenty different flavors. Use the bare minimum of ingredients. If you're out of something, that's fine you can probably live without it, unless it's onion.

SANDWICH SYSTEM

Sandwiches are one of the most significant technological developments since the dawn of man. They can be eaten without a plate or cutlery. They can be eaten with one hand while walking, driving, or even riding a bike (if you're good). Sandwiches can contain the entire food pyramid in one sandwich and be a significantly easier shape to carry and consume.

They generally have protein, sometimes cheese, always carbs, and leafies even if you're so inclined. They can be partially eaten and saved for later, nibbled on bit by bit, and with the help of a ziploc bag can be conveniently placed in the large pouch of a carpenter's bags for on demand nibbling while on the job. They can be eaten hot or cold. They can be heated on the dashboard of a car or truck on a sunny day, or wrapped in tinfoil and placed on a hot engine block. They can be served with soup, salad, french fries, or with nothing at all. Their portability and versatility make them among popular lunch foods in the world. From the hamburger to the grilled cheese, to the french dip, to the ruben, to the philly cheesesteak, to the montecristo; sandwiches have played a major part in the development of the modern world as we know it.

Subs, Shrimp Po-boys, steak sandwiches, salmon burgers, meatloaf sandwiches, sloppy joes, and tuna fish sandwiches all have one thing in common: greatness. Making a dent in sandwich history is I'm sure a dream of many of you as well, but in a world where it's all been done, I've resigned myself to simply improving the process in a way that helps me get through the week without succumbing to the temptation of someone else's sandwiches, instead of one built with my own two hands. Welcome to Sandwich System.

I build systems to refine efficiency and eliminate waste of time, money, and resources in our lives. Sandwich System is no exception.

Mornings have the potential to be hectic , especially in households with children. In our house, I'm the early riser. My wife has struggled with coffee addiction since she was a small child (in Guatemala they start em young) and at this point, rather than trying to find a way for her to kick the filthy habit, I'm tempted to just enable her early enough that she's able to get out of bed in time to get the kids to school before the bell rings. This means that every day it's my job to wake up and make coffee, take the dog out for potty time, make breakfast, make lunches, and hopefully, if there's time, we all walk to drop the boys off at school and my wife and I can continue on to the futile chore of giving our boxer pup Boteneta enough exercise as to not drown us in her emotional neediness for the rest of the day.

The sandwich system is useful in our regular daily routine, but works out differently depending on where we are because in Guatemala we only eat fresh bread that's delivered every morning and don't buy sandwich bread. When we're here in the United States, we generally use sliced bread, as is the custom here and at least there is a good selection. When in Rome, do as the Romans do, I guess.

Sandwich System works like this. Imagine you have to make ten pepperoni, ham, bologna, cheese, sandwiches on swirl rye. Obviously that's twenty pieces of bread, ten pieces of cheese, ten pieces of bologna, ten pieces of ham; plus pickles, greens, dijon mustard, mayo, salt, and pepper. Your hard costs are basically fixed no matter how you slice it. Your time is the only variable. If you were to sit down and make all of them, one by one, you would start to get better around the third sandwich, gaining an efficiency advantage, but there is still room to improve. If you made them at separate times that would be the worst because you'd be washing your knife in between sandwiches and never getting in the groove as you got practice. Sandwich system is about scaling up your sandwich game so as to pre-prepare to the degree that you have sandwiches at your immediate disposal, at all times, like a life sized pez-dispenser, but for sandwiches.

You make all ten at once, and you use a silicone spatula to spread the mayo and mustard, just like the pros do. First you spread all the mayo on all the pieces of bread that get Mayo. Then you wipe your spatula and spread all of the mustard on the slices of bread that get mustard. You do each process for all the sandwiches one at a time. Eventually you are laying down turkey or ham and ready to close them up. You make them all and then you carefully stack them up and put them back into the same bag that the bread came in. So now, instead of having a loaf of bread, you have a loaf of sandwiches. Now place that loaf of sandwiches in the fridge.

When someone needs to go to school and wants a sandwich, take one out and serve it up. Boom. When someone needs to go to work and wants a sandwich, pack it up, boom! Let's say you come home from work for lunch.

That's easy, drop a little butter into a small frying pan, shake and dump the soup into a bowl and start the microwave, drop the sando into the pan and Boom! Soup and a crispy hot sandwich ... Boom. This is a five minute endeavor and you'd be hard pressed to get a better product anywhere that quickly for any price.

Look, in the end it's all about preparation. Luck favors the prepared, as they say. Whether it's the Soup System or the Sandwich System, it's about scheduling: schedule the time to make the soup and make the sandwiches when you have time and when it's most therapeutic for you. This way you are killing two birds with one stone instead of running around like a chicken with its head cut off. If you're trying to achieve the same end but it's unplanned and you're in a hurry, the product won't turn out as well, or you'll skip it all together and go with a more expensive, lower quality alternative.

SAVE MORE
OR
EARN MORE?
OR BOTH?

Benjamin Franklin coined the phrase, a penny saved is a penny earned. In truth, it's actually more. You pay taxes on the money you earn. Money you save is tax free. In the most extreme examples you can put virtually all of your money to productive use, wasting virtually none of it. But you can not save more than you earn.

At this point, we've covered most of the low lying fruit: don't try to impress everyone with brand new vehicles when you can buy like new, or shun the concept of impressing anyone at all and buy used for what could end up being a 20X savings. Wonderful clothes are available for pennies on the dollar and no one will know the difference. Oh, and you'll blow up your credit cards by eating out at restaurants and you don't need to if you only take the responsibility of feeding yourself and your family for yourself.

Those three categories are the main places people are messing up their financial lives. From the exterior, their lives seem perfect: great job, cool car, nice clothes, enjoying life; the perfect image of success and prosperity. The reality is often: high stress, overworked, credit card debt, constant arguing about money, and the cruel weight of knowing that you're not really living truthfully with the people that are close to you.

The concern that your new affluent friends won't accept you if they knew the truth about your mounting credit card debt, your leased vehicles, and the horrible secret about how you've mismanaged your money so badly. Being one economic catastrophe away from losing everything is too much stress for the average person to handle and can lead to other problems that can affect your marriage, family life, and happiness in general. Don't worry too much about your new affluent friends, it's highly likely they are doing the same thing as you are.

If this is you, start to employ techniques that break you away from your old habits. If you have a problem with credit cards, cutting them up is not a bad idea. Order new copies for emergencies after you've made progress paying them down for six consecutive months. After six months of restraint you will have better self discipline and might be able to trust yourself to put one of them back in your wallet, but it's probably better to just keep them in your desk drawer. Make it inconvenient for you to fall into your old ways. You don't need any more shoes. Repeat after me: "I don't need any more shoes."

Like any addict, you'll need something to fill the time you used to spend overspending. Make your new hobby picking up the basics of thrift. It's fun and it's trending. The whole world is finding itself in a position to be less wasteful and replace careless spending with more thoughtful pursuits, like developing skills that improve the quality of your family's life. You'll get quite a bit more satisfaction out of your life if you more purposefully direct it toward improving the lives of your family and the people around you.

You can pick up mechanical skills that will reduce your transportation costs. You can learn skills that will keep your home better maintained and avoid expensive maintenance and home improvement costs. You could pick up a gardening hobby that will eventually result in having a green thumb and end up growing higher quality produce than you could buy at the supermarket ... regardless of what prices and inflation do.

You could also upgrade the career you are already engaged in. If you work for someone else, think about how you can earn them more money. If you have your own business, think about how you can deliver more value to your customers. Work is about providing value to other people, and the better you do that the more money you are likely to make. If you have free time, consider a side hustle that solves a common problem. The more common the problem, the easier it will be to sell your product or service. Put yourself in the right mindset to be of service to others for profit, and the universe will reward you in time.

HIDE YOUR MONEY (FROM YOURSELF)

Having money is one of the most liberating feelings there is. If you need something, you get it. If you're not sure if you need something, you might think about it a bit more and get it just in case, and sometimes you forget to check up on that situation meaning you might have gotten something you actually didn't need, out of an abundance of caution. Whoops, oh well, it's just money, which is like water you scoop out of the stream when you need it. The easier it is to earn, the easier it is to waste. The more appropriate thing to do, if you like and respect money, is to use it as effectively as possible, conserving as much as you can, and putting it to work in some investment that will later return more money to you.

If you find yourself with extra money, as often happens as your career matures, be careful having too much of it lying around. Your hard won attitude of frugality will soften and you will begin to slowly waste more and more money buying things you don't need and indulging daily on things you could definitely live without. If it seems like you have an abundance it can feel nice to be a big spender after a lifetime of necessary thrift, but unless you're actually wealthy, you should probably put that new extra money into an investment, if nothing else, just to keep you from spending it on frivolities.

The idea is that you know how much money you need to live. You've been living on a certain amount for years. Call this your monthly minimum nut. You want to stay at that minimum as long as you can and supplement it with tricks and life hacks that improve your quality of life. Upgrade your lifestyle with the knowledge you learn: your new cooking abilities, your new green thumb, your new found taste and sophistication that prepares for picnics and fun outings that don't cost hardly anything to pull off. Don't upgrade your life by spending more money, or at least not until you actually become wealthy. Take your extra money out of your hands so it can't be spent.

Since taking money away from yourself can be psychologically difficult to do, automate it where you can. Make automatic deposits into your stock portfolio. Deposit at least one of your monthly paychecks directly into your savings account and transfer from there to something productive, at the very least a CD that returns some amount of interest. If you don't own the house you live in, buy one. If you have credit card debt, for god sakes, pay your balances down to zero every single month.

The idea is to take any extra money you might have and put it somewhere where you can't spend it, and really it should go somewhere it can not just accumulate, but also earn. It's just too difficult to try to maintain the discipline to have a big pile of cash staring you in the face every day and to not touch it. Just have the discipline to put it away somewhere safe where you can't touch it, and try to forget about it.

In my business, payments go into my business account and I pay myself my minimum monthly nut as an automatic transfer to my personal account, and another automatic transfer to my savings. I then have an automatic contribution to my stock portfolio that pulls from my savings account. Then it will accumulate there, sometimes earning as it does, and I can remove it when I have a better investment to contribute to. This way I can make sure my business stays profitable because I'm getting paid a salary from it and I don't think I'm making more than I am because of the weird fluctuations in my business account that can make it hard to tell where I'm really at.

Building our houses in Guatemala worked perfectly this way. We bought the lot with money I took out of my stock account, and sent two thousand a week down to our builder for almost a year. We didn't have money for shopping sprees or fancy vacations because the money had been committed to something else. We just did what we had been before, took picnics to the waterfall, or packed lunches for hikes or small adventures with our new baby boy. That was a great year. We didn't want for anything and at the end of it we had a beautiful house in a beautiful country.

That house is a critical part of my retirement plan because living expenses are so low down there and quality of life is so good. It's also useful to collect the Airbnb income. It worked so well, a couple of years later we did the same thing, but for a bigger, more beautiful house. Now we're Airbnb superhosts and the income makes a real difference. If we keep rolling it back over on itself, there might be a time in the future where it won't make sense for us to be this frugal anymore.

Be Flexible

There's a Buddhist principle that the root of all suffering comes from the attachment of outcome. If you're upset because your tomato plants froze, it's because you were attached to the idea that they would survive. They have a parable about how a man's son broke his arm and the man replied, that's fine. The neighbors were appalled, insisting that it was instead horrible. The next day the army came through and took all the able bodied young men to go and fight in a war and the man's son was spared. Similar things happen throughout the story to hammer down the point. The concept being that none of us have any idea what the universe has in store for us.

It's ok to have goals and desires for things to be a certain way, but we have to be able to let go of those attachments to outcome without too much emotional turmoil if we want to be available for the next opportunity around the corner.

Cultivating a flexible attitude will help you to capitalize on little opportunities along the way. When I do a quick pass at Grocery Outlet I don't have any particular meals in mind when I do it. That would cause me to miss out on any deals that don't magically align with the preconceived notion in my head. I look for the amazing deals and then I think about what else I have or will need to get them to work. The two pound pack of pepperoni I scored for 2.99 has made an excellent addition to our fridge. When it runs out, I'm not going to go and get more and the usual 12.99 price, I'l just move onto the next deal. This keeps me paying bargain prices and adds some welcome variety to our selections.

Going to the store to buy for a particular recipe is a sure way to walk out without getting any deals. I plan meals in the opposite direction: I find a deal, and then I figure out what to make with it. It helps that I have years of experience doing it this way and the skills to pull it off, but even the novice cook could find a bargain and look up recipes with that item as its main ingredient. This is actually the correct way to do it and it has always been this way.

In the old days markets didn't have the wonderful and consistent selection that they do today. It was more like the street markets my wife and I shop at in Guatemala.

"Oh look," my wife will say, "the fish guy is here today and he has octopus". Now we just need to make sure we have garlic and figure out what else we're going to serve with it.

If you go late in the day to the Antigua market berries, mushrooms, and leafy greens are all available for bargain prices because they are so perishable that they won't last long enough to be sold the following day. In that case, it looks like we'll be freezing berries for smoothies and picking up some meat that we can have with our mushroom sauce and a green salad with sliced mushrooms.

Flexibility and an open mind means you can take advantage of opportunities and will sometimes fill you with a thankful wonder that serendipity could provide so well on such short notice.

One time an old friend of mine was in town and had rented a beautiful room in a new vacation property that had been recently built. By coincidence I had installed all the windows in that property, all five hundred and eighty of them, but that's beside the point. He wanted to make Spaghetti Carbonara for dinner because he wanted to show me the recipe because it was a lifesaver for him in college because it was cheap and filling and delicious.

Carbonara got its name from the coal (Carbon) miners that used to eat it because it's cheap and filling and delicious. We went to the store and got a pack of spaghetti, a small package of bacon, a tiny bottle of olive oil, a small bundle of parsley, a small little six-pack of eggs, and a tiny bottle of parmesan cheese. Luckily the hotel/timeshare thing he was staying at had salt and pepper or he would have had to buy that too. By the time we got up to the checkstand and paid, it was twenty one Dollars! We didn't even get any wine, which is customary to drink with carbonara, just ask any coal miner. This was back around 2010, so in today's dollars it would be something more like forty dollars.

Even at twenty dollars we had completely invalidated Carbonara's primary purpose: to be cheap, in addition to filling and delicious. It's because we went in there with a fixed mindset and absolutely had to have all of those things. In the end it was worth it because we were still saving a bundle over eating out, and I got to learn how to make it which has saved me a ton of money over the years.

PICNIC POWER

Being thrifty so you can save money for investments to make your retirement more comfortable doesn't have to be boring. Who says frugality isn't sexy? Ninety nine percent of women that's who. Nothing turns a woman on more than wasting a ton of money on her. It only works if you have so much money that you can actually afford to do it without injuring yourself financially. That's the appeal from the eyes of the woman, spending it so carelessly must mean you have a ton of it. If you throw a bunch of money around, spending it carelessly, and it later comes to light that you actually don't have very much and were being particularly unwise to spend it so foolishly, that can be seen as a bit of a red flag.

The trick for any young single men that might be reading: frugality is about being realistic about your current station, sensible about the way you derive value from your labors, and ambitious about your future and the focused path you charted to achieve that. You want to find a girl that respects those values and can work together with you to achieve those goals. Avoid the other ones like the plague. If you do manage to find one that can help you with your plans, make her your wife. It's the most important part of your mission because if you choose wrong it will be a major setback that is very hard to recover from.

If you are wooing a possible suitor, or wooing your wife, which by the way is a never ending ambition all married men must constantly achieve, maintain, and periodically re-achieve; there is not a more time tested technique than the picnic. It demonstrates your ability to plan, pack, provide, and pick a wonderful location, and it shows your willingness to dedicate your time to your woman, something they require with an unending appetite. For us, it's a family institution.

I'll gather up some Grocery Outlet scores: salami, crackers, cheeses, a bottle of wine (don't forget the opener and two wine glasses); off we'll go, into the wild blue yonder, to some spot I'd recently discovered or know about for years. The kids will run around and explore and my wife and I will spend an hour or two enjoying eachothers company on what's usually a Saturday or Sunday. My wife doesn't care that the salami is from Grocery Outlet and I paid less than half price, but then again that's probably because our financial lives are tied at the hip and me wasting money on her is still a waste, especially if we can have the same thing for half the money.

Picnics are not good for first dates because women have security concerns that mean you need to earn some of their trust before you try to take them somewhere secluded. But if after the second or third date you feel a connection and want to share your enthusiasm for one of your favorite outdoor spots, it's best to ask her permission if it's ok for you to take her somewhere where you can enjoy nature. Don't say anything about the picnic, surprises are better received and it's always better to under-promise and over deliver.

If the salami, the cheese, and the wine are all good and well paired, and the scenery spectacular, and your date is cranky that you didn't take her somewhere fancy instead, perhaps it means that she lacks the class to enjoy god's bounty and is busy fulfilling some ego trip instead. Run away as fast as you can and re-focus your efforts on someone who likes the same things as you.

I'm not really the right person to be giving dating advice, and really this book is more focused on how young couples and families can waste less money to help them to achieve their more long term financial goals. Therefore, I can't recommend enough the value of picnics, not necessarily strictly as a romantic endeavor, but just as a way to enjoy the company of your family in a simple unadulterated way. Yes you could go to a movie, or to a trampoline park, or a restaurant, and you should do all those things too, in moderation; but for my family, enjoying just each other, with some nice snacks, in a beautiful setting; is a very grounding experience and offers some clarity and piece of mind that more commercial activities lack. There is something wonderful about having a great time with your wife and children and never once needing to take your wallet out.

MUNICIPAL RESOURCES

Coming back from Guatemala I've come to really appreciate the quantity of public parks, libraries, recreation centers, swim centers, and the multitude of municipal resources available to residents of most cities and towns in the United States. I think it's easy for many Americans to forget how wonderful that is. In Guatemala we have tons of fun stuff for families to do, but … you have to pay for it. There are restaurants that have wonderful playgrounds, open spaces, and beautiful vistas for families to enjoy, but they might have a problem with me setting up my picnic on one of their tables. The expectation is that the facilities are available to use for paying customers, as evidenced by the sign, "No Outside Food or Drink".

While I'm certainly glad free enterprise has provided for these wonderful resources, I can't help but miss the United States and the plethora of available resources, available to use often free of charge. The swim center here in Gardnerville, Nevada charges six dollars for one adult and one child, so it's twelve for the family, but it's an incredible facility and there's no time limit on your stay. It's got a kids pool and waterslides and a warm water physical therapy pool, in addition to an olympic sized pool for laps and another for diving. Twelve dollars isn't free, but it's quite reasonable and makes for a nice adventure when the kids need to burn off some energy. The community pool we have in Guatemala is free for all residents who pay the $35/mo HOA fees, and it's great, but a little quaint compared to the Gardnerville Swim Center.

If you're American, Canadian, or European; you've probably got tons of resources at your disposal and you should make it a point to explore all of them to see which ones appeal to yourself, your family, and your kids. If you have kids, library time is critical. It gets them out of the house, modern libraries have lots more than just books to keep the kids entertained for one or two hour blocks, and you can rent books for free, something that in my opinion is an important part of our inheritance as Americans.

My family has been exploring the local parks nearby and have been pleasantly surprised to discover there are a bunch of great parks, all very close, and well liked by our boys. They've all got new modern playground equipment and big open spaces where the boys can kick their soccer ball and run around and burn the energy they would otherwise use to annoy myself, my wife and eachother.

They are like our Boxer puppies, if we don't run them, their behavior suffers, which means we suffer. My wife has a similar disposition: she can not spend an entire day inside the house, or her attitude will suffer. If I'm at work then she'll take the boys for different adventures: to the park, to the library, for walks. On the weekends is usually when we'll do the Swim Center or maybe the municipal shooting range (you gotta love Nevada). The trick is to stay out of stores and paid entertainment as much as possible, so that when you do spend on those types of activities at least it's appreciated.

Absence makes the heart grow fonder

My kids get excited for top-ramen for dinner. You must be asking yourself how I was able to achieve such a magical situation? They'll jump up and down for mac and cheese too. It's not because they are the type of kids that only eat mac and cheese, quite the opposite. The variety of food they eat is second to none. Our boys are regularly complimented on their willingness to anything that's put in front of them. This was carefully cultivated by giving them a wonderful selection of food to eat as they were growing up, in the years before kids get picky; and then later by not caving to their picky tendencies and responding with, "Well, that's what we're having tonight so if you don't want to eat it, you don't have to, but I won't be making anything else."

They eat everything we give them because the food we make is good, and they don't have any other choice.

They don't grow tired of meals, because between my wife and I, our catalog of meals is extensive, and we're regularly trying new things and skilled enough generally to pull it off on the first try. Variety is the spice of life. It keeps life feeling fresh and food is so important to human morale, regardless of the situation: slaves, soldiers, workers, or prisoners; good food is one thing that will maintain optimism and hope in the most dire of circumstances.

It goes not just for food, but also for activities. If all you ever do is go to the movies, your kids won't be very impressed when you take them to the movies, and kids unlike romantic dates, will make no accounting for how much you spent to entertain them. Also, if you're always going to movies you're likely to see a few duds, thus burning some enthusiasm for the theater in general.

We rarely go to the theater, but when we do, it's for a guaranteed hit, something you would want to see in the theater for impact. Most movies can be enjoyed quite effectively from your own home theater, so I save the silver screen for only the sure-things that require that large format for their spectacular nature. To be honest, the rarity of going to the movie theater has raised the expectations of the experience so much that I'm pretty disappointed if the movie is anything less than outstanding.

If I suspect that a movie might be less than outstanding, we don't go. That saves us seventy five to a hundred dollars and we can do something else instead. My wife is good about paying attention to local Facebook notifications. The truth is that there are more events than we can go to, especially if you count all the commercial events like new movies and business openings.

If you live in America, there should be no challenge in showing your kids new experiences. There will be mainstreet parades, highschool football (soccer, basketball, baseball, volleyball) games, highschool and junior college theater, orchestra, and special guest performances. It's true, not all of them will be world class performances, but your young children will be dazzled. Older children might require a ride to the nearest university to be dazzled, but it can't be that far away and as long as you don't do it all the time, there will be some curious novelty in the experience.

ATTITUDE IS EVERYTHING

In the end it all depends how you, your wife, and your kids deal with your new approach to spending money. Best would be if they couldn't perceive the goal at all and instead be pleasantly surprised with your new life of outings, adventure, and quality family time. Most people spend so much time worrying about their debt and showing off to neighbors that they're not very present for their kids anyway. What if you converted to a new system of spending time with your family instead of taking what seems like the easy way out by just spending money?

It's easy to get caught up in the drudgery of work and simply follow the slightest suggestion of the radio on the way home from work, or the TV, or suggestions that your children might have absorbed from the various forms of media that they might have been exposed to throughout the day. It's about planning, remember? That means you constantly need to have a better activity planned so you don't get pinned into doing the neatest thing that your family heard of at that moment. Paintball tonight? That's a good idea for another day, but dad already has plans for catfish noodling (or whatever equally exciting adventure is customary for your area). Keep a couple of winners in your back pocket in case one of your family members catches you off guard with a zinger that could derail your whole program of thrift and a more pure life that savors the simple pleasures.

Attitude is everything but it takes time to cultivate the right attitude. You want to cultivate a spirit of adventure in yourself and in the different members of your family but not all souls have the same acceptance and aptitude for adventure. As the father you are the de facto leader and must lead by example. Build in enough time and tolerance into your system to cultivate the qualities that will help your family to convert from housecat urbanites into the country woods creatures that can entertain themselves with their own ingenuity and god's gifts alone. Lead them with baby steps to build their confidence little by little until they can come to appreciate the adventures you provide. You'll know when it's working when they use their phones to take pictures to post and show to their friends instead of blindly sifting through the media they see online.

Take the time and be willing to spend the gas to do adventures that require effort and stamina as this cultivates an appreciation for things here in the natural world. Your kids will have plenty of time occupying the virtual world, make sure you're able to have fun with them here in real life, and they get some practice having fun IRL (newspeak for In Real Life). Kids are getting incredible amounts of screen time and now since much of their school work and instruction is also online, it takes making a real effort to get them outside and into IRL social situations that will allow them to develop what we old folks that grew up without the internet would consider normal social behavior, not the awkward neurotic social anxiety that appears to be the new normal for teens, tweens, and young adults these days.

It's important to remember what you are saving your money for. Sometimes you'll be so effective at being thrifty that you'll cross the rubicon into territory normally known as stingy. You're being thrifty so that you can remove the waste that robs you of your earnings and burdens you with unnecessary stress. Being frugal doesn't mean never spending money on anything fun. It means cutting out the unnecessary spending so you can live the life that's closer to what you really want.

MAKE A TRADE

For example, let's say you have a starbucks habit that between the coffee and the muffins puts you at about ten dollars a day. While I enjoy a good coffee as much as the next person, seventy dollars a week is quite the budget and might be put to better use. Make a coffee at home instead and you've got two hundred and eighty dollars per month to buy coffee and muffins at the store with and save the remainder for let's say, a ski trip for the family. On the year, that's three thousand, six hundred, and fifty dollars, minus coffee and muffins you buy at the store for your house.

With money like that you could book an airbnb for a couple of nights in February up in Tahoe and plan on shelling out for tickets and rental gear. If you're buying ski gear for the whole family it's going to blow right through your thirty six hundred bucks real fast so you'll have to employ some frugality still to turn that starbucks money into an awesome family experience.

Either rent the snow clothes or swing into a thrift store in the ski town you're staying in and you'll find a nice assortment lightly used snow clothes, hats, helmets, goggles, and even skis; but I'd recommend getting set up at the rental store with modern gear so that you're not fussing about in the morning trying to piece together equipment instead of enjoying the slopes. It might be even cheaper to buy used gear than to rent, but you want to make sure that you can assemble the whole kit and that everything is sized correctly, so in that case the rental shop might be a better option, depending on what you find.

You can wash all the ski clothes at the airbnb the night before so they are ready for the morning. Also, try not to get any big ambitions about buying gear and coming back again and again. Wait until you get a total on the weekend before you take on any more obligations, like storing ski equipment. If you decide you like it and can afford to do it more than once a year, you can always come back next year and try to find gear for everyone.

For now let's just get up on the mountain and see if everyone can have a good time. If you don't know how to ski, don't forget to budget for lessons. They will cost you an arm and a leg so see if you can book a freelance private instructor ahead of time by asking around in ski groups on facebook, but if you can't find one, bite the bullet and get one or two days of instruction because if you don't have fun after all the expense you've gone to, you've thrown out the baby with with bathwater.

Seven hundred for the Airbnb, two hundred for ski clothes for a family of four, six hundred for rentals, four hundred for lessons, eight hundred for lift tickets, and two hundred for gas. That's twenty nine hundred before meals so eat breakfast and dinner at the airbnb and bring sandwiches up to the mountain. Plan on fifty bucks for hot coco and french fries at the lodge, unless you're clever enough to pack a thermos of coco and or soup ahead of time. Hey, I never said skiing was cheap, but an experience like that is something your family will never forget and it puts that Starbucks habit in perspective. If you cut back on the wasteful spending you can put it into something more fun.

If you do it right, your kids won't think of you as a cheapskate. If you're often doing fun trips like that they're not going to beef you on the details. They'll probably notice that you don't like to throw money away on stupid things, but if you recycle those savings into providing fun experiences for them, they'll respect you all the more for doing it. Hopefully they'll make those same thrifty values part of their own value set and use them when they have their own family. In the end it's about not being wasteful, and that's a great lesson to pass on to your children.

The Environmental Case Against Wastefulness

While it's certainly trendy to put on airs about your love of the environment and willingness to do things to save it, most people put on a big show about it while completely missing the point. Notice how their love of the environment and nature always fits in neatly with consumerism. Nobody wants to do things to protect the environment unless they outwardly show, and the way they show better be sparkling clean and wreak of money. It's usually some kind of status play like, "I bought this new car to save the environment", or "we went on a trip to patagonia to save the penguins". What a bunch of tools.

It's always outward value signaling that does nothing to save the environment but instead is all about saving face with their fake friends that also have no interest in actually saving the environment. "Saving the environment" usually has something to do with consuming less resources, which doesn't jive very well with consumerism, which is the thing that all these jokers are consistently addicted to.

Buying a new patagonia jacket every year for the whole family is actually quite wasteful. If they were really interested in saving the environment, they would try to consume as little as possible, not rush out and buy new stuff all the time because the Jones family next store did and they don't want to look like they are falling behind.

These same people will support the banning of plastic straws because they saw a photo of a sea turtle with one sticking out of its nose, and then turn around and throw a glitter party to celebrate one more win against microplastics contaminating the environment. Their lack of self awareness is an epic unfunny comedy and this confederacy of dunces produce children that are likely to confront your children at school about why they don't have the latest trend in bento-box lunchbox with four disposable double seal zip-loc bags just for snack time.

If you actually care about the environment and try to be as least wasteful as possible, you will inevitably face pushback from the insufferable wine-moms that make it their personal life mission to enforce conformity in their neighborhoods and children's schools.

The irony is that they will bully you on the grounds that you are destroying the environment while they are protecting it when quite the opposite is true. This is where it's best to rest in the solace knowing your own ass from a hole in the ground, something your intellectual opponents can not boast. Engaging with these idiots is a fruitless endeavor. I believe it was Mark Twain who said, "Never argue with a stupid person. They will bring you down to their level and beat you with experience". It's never been more true.

The funny thing is you don't need much of an education in environmental science to be more kind to the environment. Infact, based on the environmental scientists that I've met personally, you might be better off without it all together. All you need to know is that consuming more products, especially things that take a lot of carbon (energy) to produce, should be minimized when possible.

Carbon-cost is a term that can be applied to different products as a way to make some sort of accounting for the amount of energy it took to create. Everything manufactured has some kind of carbon cost, and even agricultural produce have some degree of carbon cost based on energy used to fertilize, harvest, and transport during production and delivery to market. Most people have no idea about any of this and just look for a little green leaf on a package before buying it.

My own mother, who views herself as some kind of champion of the environment (yes, the same person that got rid of the perfectly working blender because she didn't like the color, to instead buy a new one every year for the last ten years and into perpetuity). She made the decision, based on her love of the environment and willingness to sacrifice to protect it, to stop buying white coffee filters and instead buy coffee filters made from unbleached paper. While her heart was definitely in the right place, the trouble is that she buys them in packages of one hundred, that come in cute little boxes made from thick cardstock. Oh, and she orders them from amazon, so they get delivered to the house, in a big truck, sometimes packed inside another box with nothing else in it, except more packaging material.

While I am not an environmental scientist, when the box weighs more than the filters, and the product was couriered directly to the the end consumer in a big truck instead of shipped to a store, and there was other packaging that had its own carbon cost associated with it; I'm pretty sure there is no carbon savings in that exchange.

Since it had appeared she had completely missed the point, I bought her a big bag of what was probably 1000 coffee filters, packaged in a plastic bag (reusable, recyclable, and better to keep the product inside from being damaged and thus wasted) and the whole bag was around three dollars which was probably close to what she had been paying for her box of one hundred coffee filters. But, because they were white, and had no little green leaf printed on the packaging, she would not use them, and continued to order more of the same she had before. I tried.

Without diving too deep into the education you would need to be a Real environmental warrior we can still outcompete all the fakers with just a few principles. The more you can use something before throwing it out, the more utility is gained from its initial carbon investment. If it then can be used by someone else, recycled and turned into something else, or biodegrade and thus return to organic production, that's also good.

The scale and efficiency with which a product is produced affects its initial carbon cost. If it's special, and for a niche market, it probably has a higher initial carbon cost than its mass produced counterpart. It also probably costs more, which brings me to my third principle: since energy to harvest raw materials, manufacture, and to deliver a product to market are significant to the cost of a product, if it costs more, it's probably more energy intensive to produce than a competing product that costs less.

The most environmentally sound thing you can do is to buy used goods. Why mine new minerals, use vast amounts of energy to smelt, melt, press, and make them into new commodities to then manufacture those commodities into new products using tools, labor, energy, and transportation. Why do that if the product still works and can still be used for its original purpose to deliver value to its user? The original buyer has already decided to move on, which might mean its other destiny is in a landfill. To save an object from the landfill and put it back into productive service is one of the most environmentally sound things you can do. Basically the best advice is "Don't be wasteful". But it doesn't mean you won't catch some guff for doing it.

Karen the wine mom has, ever since she got her new Tesla, been working on her self-righteous snicker for just the moment when she passes you and the other parents driving gas vehicles in the line to pick up the kids from school. She literally has nothing else to do with herself and for some reason gets some kind of value out of asserting her environmental virtuousness over the other moms and dads that don't drive Teslas or wear this year's patagonia. Don't let it get to you.

If you're affected by her vacuous self loathing, you'll need a self confidence tune up and to reaffirm the conviction that you know what you are doing with your family and finances and are correct according to your own values and goals. You are not dependent on the approval of twit morons for satisfaction of your own self image and esteem. You know what you are doing is right, for you, your family, and the environment; and their ignorant, self-important, rude, and hypocritical status game is for the birds and doesn't affect you in any way unless you let it.

Don't cave to social pressure and buy into the status game that is the rat race. Liberate yourself from all of that by disregarding the Karrens for what they are: ignorant, self involved, and unhappy people. Pay them no mind. Instead, do what Jesus would do (not the gardener, the lord), turn the other cheek and bless their little hearts. They're probably just stressed because the Tesla payments, electricity bill (from charging the Tesla), and REI credit card payments are all coming due at the same time.

Build Your Own Community

It's important for you to build your own community around the values that are important to you and your family. You don't want your kids to catch any flack for not having this year's patagonia jackets, at least not with the kids they play with after school. At school, they're subject to the same kind of bullying you find from Karen and the likes, and we must all know how to disregard that type of attention when it comes around. Hopefully you don't deal with it often, I don't, or maybe I just don't notice when it does. It depends where you are and what the pretentiousness index is in your particular area, but regardless of where you are, you'll want to build a community around you with people that share your values, including your value of thrift.

In my opinion, it's actually an important value and I've found it to be pretty central to having meaningful relationships. It's almost like there are two types of people: those that value and respect the value of money, and those that are putting on airs about how successful and important they are and basically faking everything about their lives as though no one can notice. I have all kinds of friends, some of which are more like professional acquaintances that I may not see perfectly eye to eye with, but I'm a pretty agreeable guy and can get along with just about anyone, sometimes it just takes a little more effort than normal.

Professional obligations will often keep us close to people that we don't necessarily see perfectly eye to eye with, but that's ok, it keeps us on our toes. When building a community you want to find people that think the same way about the important things. Don't get too picky because you don't want to end up in an echo chamber like Karen and her friends. It's really only the important things that we are worried about as parents. Respect for thrift, this way we are not at odds about where to meet or what to do. If your friends are inviting you to the Cayman Islands, make sure they've offered to pay, or at least know you are not in a position to live that type of lifestyle.

Your close friends should be people that live the same way you do. They'll invite you over for a barbecue, or for dinner and a movie in their living room. If they want to go out on the town to blow a few hundred dollars on cocktails at swanky night spots, they are in that case apparently not on the 'thrift to invest in our future' program. Maybe it's fun to go out a few times, and hopefully that will suit your goals in some way, otherwise it will be like you're following a path that doesn't suit you because you are lonely and haven't found your group yet.

Trying to fit into a place you don't belong is a bit of a fool's errand. Eventually you will be found out. With the level of fakery you find in today's society, it might even be more likely that all the friends you were going out with were all faking it together, and eventually the whole thing will extinguish the way a fire does when it runs out of fuel, or in this case, money.

Your own personal community are the people that are important in your own life, regardless of their geographical location. It's amazing how little physical location matters in today's world. My friends are all over the county and all over the globe. Sometimes we'll keep in touch better when we are far away than when we are close, which I admit is an artifact of failing to prioritize time with the people closest to you. Best is to take advantage of times when people you care about are close in location, so you can do things together in person.

Our family's lifestyle is a bit unusual at the moment. We live between two places that are very far apart and most of our friends live between those two places, and some in other far away places. When we visit Tahoe, we like to visit the friends we have here, and do trips to our friends that live out of the area but still close enough to drive to.

When we are in Guatemala, we have a different set of friends. Most are fairly close by and we do our best to see everyone we can while we're around, but I have to admit that the schedule of maintaining our social relationships can be a bit intense. My wife is a bit of a social butterfly and therefore has a huge social network, but she does have good taste in people and it's a pleasure to keep up with everyone, even if it can be a bit exhausting at times.

Not all of your friends are going to see perfectly eye to eye with you on the value of money, and what you are comfortable spending to meet each other. Antigua Guatemala is a fancy place with no shortage of fancy restaurants and bars. Meeting at a swanky place for some drinks or a bite to eat might end up costing upwards of a hundred dollars. When I'm working in the United States for big money and just visiting Guatemala for a short time, I'm happy to live it up and spend money. I'm less inclined when we are staying for longer periods or don't have a full calendar of work lined up for the near future. It's always good to have an alternative ready in case an impromptu visit approaches with the prospect of evaporating a couple of hundred dollars just to hang out for an hour or two.

I don't mind spending good money for something exceptional. My wife is a fan of fine things so I'm sure to take her somewhere nice for birthdays and anniversaries. My criteria is that I take her somewhere really nice: where both the food and the service is outstanding. Like the kind of stuff we can't do at home.

If I spend sixty dollars on a steak it doesn't bother me if it's good. We don't do it very often and for the rest of my life I can close my eyes and remember how delicious that steak was. I can also learn what I can from the experience to see if I can reproduce those results when I'm at home. It's good to experience fine things, but in moderation and within the bounds of your own financial circumstances.

Certain friends might not want to meet at your house for drinks or a cheese plate, or to make pizzas or any of the fun offerings you have. I would always prefer to have guests over than to meet at a restaurant or bar where we are almost certain to spend a fortune and deal with other inconveniences like the music being too loud to effectively communicate with our friends. Nonetheless, sometimes it makes the most sense and in those cases I prefer to at least negotiate for a place that even if it isn't cheap, is good and justifies the premium prices they command. In that case, we dress up and enjoy our night on the town. I utilize opportunities like that to treat my wife to a special night, considering how she tolerates my thriftiness the rest of the time.

In Guatemala we have a maid, and this makes entertaining friends and a no brainer. If people bring their own drinks, all we have to do is make the food and do a little cleanup before bed. It's easy and fun and costs me less than going to a restaurant even if we split the check. We like to throw pizza parties.

We'll make a bunch of dough ahead of time so that it has time to rise. A bag of shredded cheese, some tomato sauce, toppings like pepperoni or my famous smoked chorizo, black olives, kalamata olives, feta cheese, bell pepper, onion, tomato and fresh basil; give us the toppings we need to make a variety of favorite pizzas. Greek pizza, Margarita, Cheese and Pepperoni for the kids, Combo, and anything else you can get out of that topping selection.

We'll make some garlic chips to make sure the oven is up to temp and serve them as appetizers. Everybody can make their own pizza which is a fun experience, in addition to being a delicious meal that leaves everyone well fed. I might look like a generous host for cooking the pizzas and providing all the ingredients, but the hidden truth is that I'm being an insufferable cheapskate who's spending less than twenty dollars to host a party, and generally getting my beer for free.

These pizza parties are so economical to host that it's something I've incorporated into our technique to avoid spending excessive time and big money in Antigua meeting friends. If we always have a pizza party planned, when old friends get in contact with us and invite us to swanky night spots in Antigua, we counter with, "We'd love to, but we are having such a busy week. Can you and your family make it to our pizza party next Saturday instead?" This way everyone gets a better value and we all have more fun... and that's the idea right?

I like to be generous, and I like to be able to afford to be generous. In this way my skills, creativity, and ability to plan are what give me what I need to be generous. If I skip one meal out I'll have the budget required to pay for all the ingredients. Part of it is that I'd rather be generous with all of my friends that attend my pizza party, than to indulge myself once at a restaurant. I get more value out of it. It might bolster our karmic outcomes, or put us in a place to get invited to more parties, or be on the receiving end of more favors; but I like it because it's fun.

It's more fun to have a pizza with a bunch of friends than to have one pizza by myself. It's more fun to watch all kids make their own pizzas and play together in the green spaces of our gated community. I'm not just generous by sharing some pizzas, we're sharing our home, we're giving fun experiences to their kids, we're sharing the peace and tranquility our gated community provides.

I don't think anyone suspects that I'm actually being thrifty when we throw these parties, but if they did, I bet they'd be able to appreciate what I'm doing, and how wonderful thrift is if it can help you to be so generous. The end result wouldn't be much different if we all met at a pizza place and ordered twelve pies. The kids wouldn't get to try out their culinary skills by making their own, and we'd have to shout to each other in a restaurant crowded with other people, and wouldn't get to choose the music or set it at the volume we prefer, but in the end we'd have approximately the same thing, plus a giant bill. So in other words, it would be the same, but not as good. And more expensive.

What we're really being generous with are our skills, creativity, and planning abilities; and I think people appreciate that even more.

Necessity is the Mother of All Invention

It's funny because I know plenty of people with money, but almost all of them are people that value thrift. I also know people that pretend to have money, have and do fancy things, but they are almost always not wealthy. In fact whatever hangup they are facing is keeping them from being wealthy because generally they are good earners that could become wealthy eventually if they could learn to quit wasting all the money they are earning. I wish those people would read this book, but it's highly likely that they will find the concept distasteful because they think thrift is a product of poverty. They don't know what I know.

Thrift might actually originate in poverty, because the people that understand it best grew up poor. Those people understand how little you actually need to live. Huntly told me that he grew up poor as a church mouse. Because of this he knew what the very bottom was like and though it didn't have much comfort, it wasn't a death sentence either. If you have a blanket to stay warm, and a biscuit to eat, that's actually enough to get through to the next day. Enough to get to the next thing. Enough to eventually build your effort into something better. That lack of comfort keeps you hungry to create more. The knowledge of the bare minimum means your willingness to endure risk is higher because you are not afraid of the bottom someone born wealthy might be.

If you were born wealthy and have never experienced poverty, it's all academic, hearsay at best. To be poor must be horrible, obviously, right? It must be cold and dark and wet and smelly with rats and disease. Real poverty, the kind you find in developing countries is in fact, pretty damn horrible. The wimpy American version is not ideal, but it's not nearly as bad as its foreign counterpart. Here in America poverty looks something like: only one parking spot, better lock up your truck, chain that bicycle out front to the railing or it will be gone by the morning. All those foods we talked about eating to save money and stay on track with investment goals, that's your day to day: rice and beans, top ramen, spaghetti, sardines and crackers for lunch, eggs and grits for dinner. It's hardly luxury but you still have hot water and an economic environment to rise up to better accommodations over time. Why do you think so many people want to immigrate here?

Don't you find that the least bit curious? Why would someone from Honduras, El Salvador, Guatemala, or Venezuela sell everything they have to come here to the USA and live in a crappy apartment next to a bunch of drug dealers and pimps? Because if you work hard and pay attention, you only have to do it for a little while.

I understand human psychology is difficult and there are all kinds of funny little nuances that come up when someone grows up poor or rich and often has certain traits as a result. Some people can't help but create the appearance that they are wealthy when in reality they are far from it. However, if you look at how immigrants come to America with literally nothing and eventually become wealthy, it's pretty obvious frugality has something to do with it. They succeed because they are good with frugality. They are good at frugality because they were born poor. In other words, they were born into it. Lucky ducks.

The System of

Generosity

One of the ways wealthy people are able to live so well is that they share their wealth with their friends, and likewise, their friends share their wealth back. They're not sharing cash but they are sharing resources. Not everyone can have a vacation property in all the places they want to go, but if you have an extensive network of well to do friends, you might find yourself being invited to use vacation properties in all kinds of fun places. It's great if you have a property of your own that you can offer, but it isn't always necessary. If you can be generous with your time, tallent, and skills; you'll find yourself receiving the same types of invitations just the same.

I've always said that the only thing better than having a boat is having a friend with a boat. Owning a boat is a bunch of maintenance for something that most likely will not get used more than a couple of times a year. Better is to be friends with someone that wants to take you out on their boat. Boats, especially sail boats, have this great feature: they require a crew to operate. First of all, it's no fun to go out on the water by yourself, and secondly, it's good to have a few extra hands on deck in case something goes wrong.

I had a friend who's family owned a popular Swiss restaurant in town. He loved to go sailing and he loved to invite people on his boat. His policy was, "Bring some snacks and beer", and he didn't mean just enough for yourself. He was a trained chef and had a little hibachi that swung out over the water and would make delicious food while someone else would captain the boat and everyone else would enjoy themselves. It worked out great because an excellent time would be had by all and he didn't even have to pay for drinks. It was a big party and all it cost him was a little bit of gas to get out of the harbor and whatever meat or veggies he might be grilling up.

I ended up on his regular crew because I knew how to sail, and I knew how to fix things. A couple times I had to clean off the battery terminals to get the boat started or fix a cabinet latch or other things to make myself useful. Plus I knew the system of making the boat ready for sale and always helped to stow the gear and the sails so my host could attend to his guests at the end of the trip. I also always brought beer. For one summer in particular we went out on the lake quite often and though it wasn't my boat, in many ways it was even better. I could even bring girls along, in fact, that was encouraged, and we'd have a wonderful time out on the lake and all it would cost me is a couple of six packs of beer.

I've always had the disposition to be helpful and quick on my feet to solve a problem, and it's always opened doors for me. My skill set makes me handy to have around and it's led me to be invited on boats, trips, and peoples weekend properties, sometimes just to give an opinion or some advice. Often people will learn that I do kitchens and bathrooms and they'll want me to see their place so we can brainstorm design ideas for their remodels. Many of those types of encounters resulted in jobs for my business that further fostered and strengthened my relationships with those people and often led to important referrals for my business. I'm invited on boat outings by my clients so often that owning a boat is the farthest thing from my mind.

Once, with my family, we were invited to a beach house in Guatemala for the weekend so that we could advise our hosts on how to get the house up on Airbnb for short term rentals. We had a great time: the kids played in the pool, we swam in the ocean, we stuffed ourselves with delicious seafood, and enjoyed the company of our hosts. Before leaving we set up their listing and gave them a crash course in hosting an Airbnb. It was a total win-win and we got a mini vacation out of the deal that didn't even cost an entire tank of gas.

Just by being fun, useful, helpful, and generous with your time, skills, and assets will open doors and encourage people you know to share what they have simply because they like you and like to hang out with you. My family doesn't spend much money on vacations because we don't go on that type of vacation. We stay in the guest rooms of people we know so we can catch up with them, and we try to be as helpful and fun as possible while we are there. We'll cook for everyone, clean up after ourselves, and make repairs or help with projects. Sometimes our hosts won't let us because they want us to feel like guests, but I often can't help myself because I like to be helpful and can't stand to sit still for too long.

We prefer to travel this way for several reasons. For starters it's more authentic. When you go to a new place and all you have is guidebooks and online reviews to guide you, you generally do the most touristic things, that often feel fake and fabricated, and generally cost a fortune and also a poor value. When we visit friends they show us the places that locals know about and value. Not only do you avoid the tourist traps that don't interest us much anyway, you don't miss the real attractions that the locals like to visit.

Your local friends will also have their favorite restaurants to recommend. I like to make as much food at the house as we can, but it's good to invite your hosts to a meal out at a place of their choosing to show appreciation for them hosting you. They are saving you a boatload of money by opening their home to you so you're still getting a great deal so don't be stingy.

The other part of this is to extend your generosity in the same way, with no expectation to receive anything in return. We love to invite people to enjoy our properties in Guatemala. If we are there at the time, we can make a room available to them in the house we live in. If the bigger house is not rented, then we give it to our guests to enjoy. It's larger and they'll enjoy the privacy of being in a separate house. It's not just about privacy for them. House guests don't like to disturb the privacy of their hosts, so it's best to alleviate that in any way you can.

One great thing about second homes, it doesn't cost you anything, except maybe cleaning, to let someone use them. That's why it's a wonderful commodity for trades and in the economy of favors. It's a little different if it's an income property. Giving up a booking incurs opportunity cost and stings a little bit more to lose hard cash coming in for a favor going out. Your guests will likely understand this and will generally be open to modifications, but if you invited them and are therefore the host, it's your responsibility to make those adjustments in a way that keeps them comfortable and satisfied.

If you don't have room for them, give them your room and stay with friends, or call in a favor with a friend that has an open property they can share as a favor to you. Do be prepared to pay that favor back, as that's a big one and only works with friends that are close and happy to help you. In the worst case scenario, put them up in a cute hotel or airbnb that you hopefully have some kind of deal or relationship with the owner so as to at least get a good deal for a last minute booking. Use the proceeds from your booking to pay for their stay and suck it up. When you offer to host someone and they go to the trouble to put things in motion to actually come and visit, you have to come through on your word. If you don't, you've invited them only to leave them stranded and they'll probably have bad feelings about that.

You will go to some expense hosting people but you should do it anyway because it's fun. Don't invite people you don't like. This whole economy of favors works on the karmic system of doing good things for people in your own personal community with no expectations. Invite people you like and want to reconnect with or want to get to know more, this way you get to enjoy your time with them and this is the value that you receive for the expenses you might incur in the process.

If you do express your generosity without expectation, only then will you receive on the other end. Sometimes friends of friends will offer to host you because you have the recommendation of mutual friends. They're doing this because they think they'll get along with you and have fun hosting you. There's many ways for karma to return the generosity you've shown to others, but the real return should be the fun you have hosting your guests. Anything else you might receive in return is a bonus.

Being thrifty does not mean misering away your precious wealth and keeping it locked up in a safe and hidden away from the world and even yourself. Thrift is about making the most of the money you earn, so that you can afford to live well and be generous with the people you care about. That should then naturally extend to thrift being a vehicle to get the most out of life.

You don't want to work your life away trying to acquire wealth you'll never enjoy, and you also don't want to be so cheap, poor, or stingy so as to not enjoy the fruits of your labor. It's fundamental to getting the most out of thrift and frugality to cultivate an appreciation for your own generosity. Being cheap and stingy makes you and your family feel poor, and really, what's the difference between living poor and being poor? The experience of both is effectively the same. Thrift should be the vehicle to making you wealthier, both in your experiences and your net worth. If it's not doing that, you're not doing it right.

BEWARE OF BOATS & RVS

Nothing screams wealth and success more than a nice boat or recreational vehicle parked in the driveway. If you truly do have enough money, and here's the kicker, enough time to use them, count yourself among the lucky. They can be a wonderful source of enjoyment for you, your family, and your friends. RVs make camping easier and more accessible than the more primitive version, and boats are just plain fun and require no explanation. The costs associated with these toys would be the only beef I have. Between maintenance, storage, winterization, and setup in the springtime, you'll be investing plenty of time and money to have the privilege of owning one.

The problem with boats and RVs is that the people that have the money to buy them often don't have the time to use them. Aside from acting as beautiful status symbols used to decorate driveways in upscale neighborhoods, I'd argue that they rarely get used as their buyers originally intended when they bought them. Buying used changes the math significantly, as it does with any vehicle, but even then it's hard to extract a good value from owning them unless you use them a lot.

The reason people that have the money to buy them generally don't have the time to use them is because those people generally have big, high stress careers or businesses that require fairly constant attention that they can't get away from very long. Jobs like that take a lot of energy and can leave their owners sapped of all remaining energy by the time the weekend comes along, leaving them not wanting to do anything.

I've always been impressed with the dads that can earn well enough to buy a bunch of gas powered toys for their kids, and then have the energy and enthusiasm to get and keep them running for weekend adventures where they need to be trailered up, transported, and at the end of the day trailered up again, returned home, and then taken out of the trailer and stowed in their places. These dads really do deserve recognition because there is no rest for them and they have hearts big enough to endure a life without rest because they are driven to provide those amazing experiences for their family.

Before you buy an RV, a boat, jetski, dirtbike, quad, or any gas powered vehicle that's just for fun, you should take some time to self reflect. Maybe you sit at a desk all day during the week and have pent up energy to burn off on the weekends. Maybe you're just a high energy person that not only doesn't mind the extra work it takes to keep those machines in working order, but loves that type of adventure and providing them to your family. Hat's off to those guys. You should also reflect about the time commitment involved in owning one of those toys.

Every time you do one of these adventure weekends, don't count on much rest. It's likely that after your weekend of recreation you'll need the following weekend to catch up on R&R and plan the next one. Don't forget that you'll need a weekend in the spring to get everything dusted off and set up, and another in the fall to get everything properly winterized and stowed for winter.

If there is winter where you live, that's three to four months out of the year where you can't use your recreational toys, and if you're into that kind of thing, you'll probably have a different set of winter toys that need to be stowed in the spring, summer, and fall. But if you are into this kind of thing, you are that high energy person and are well aware of the effort involved to keep it all going. But, if you're just thinking of getting into that lifestyle, you should try before you buy to make sure you've got the constitution for that kind of thing.

Judging by the sheer quantity of RVs and boats that I see, it would appear permanently parked in peoples yards, tells me that many of those owners originally misjudged either the time or the effort required to use those things. I'm sure that's why the second hand market for these types of things is so plentiful and relatively more affordable. I'm not poo-pooing the idea of owning an RV, boat, or any of these fun gas powered toys. An RV or travel trailer is a fun way to camp, and it's like a spare mother-in-law unit on wheels when it's not being used for camping. They're great and they're fun, but they are definitely not going to save you any money, quite the opposite.

The reason why toys like that are status symbols is because you have to be a high-earner to have them. Furthermore, you have to be an independent high-earner that somehow has the time to enjoy them; truly a position worthy of sincere envy. Don't let your envy confuse you into thinking the object will deliver the lifestyle. You will need to have the means to provide for that lifestyle, BEFORE you buy the object. If you've got the money and your financial life is in perfect order, and you've got the time to utilize something like an RV, travel trailer, or boat; by all means, go for it! They are super fun and provide a great experience for families lucky enough to have them.

On the other hand, if you have any stress associated with existing financial burdens including providing for a comfortable retirement, taking on another financial burden with a time price tag is highly unlikely to improve your situation.

Don't despair, it doesn't mean you can't have a bucket list adventure with your family, let's just take a moment to look at your options. Pretty basic travel trailers start in the high thirty thousands and go up from there. Let's say you get a pretty good deal on a nice one and pay forty thousand. You finance it for sixty months at eight percent which gives you a monthly payment of about eight hundred dollars before insurance. You would need a vehicle to tow it with, but let's assume you already have one.

At eight hundred dollars a month, you would have to use it quite a bit to get any good value out of it. Yes, you only have to make the payments for five years and after that it's yours to keep, but after five years you'll need to fuss with what might be some pretty expensive repairs. The old way of camping only required a tent, some sleeping bags, and a camp stove if you were fancy; but I understand these are different things. If you're thinking about how you'll get value out of it after it's paid off, buy one that's five years old and you'll save a bundle, but also have to deal with higher maintenance expenses. If you're buying a new one it's because you value the purported trouble free nature of it.

How many days a month do you intend to camp? Two weekends a month seems pretty ambitious to me. Also, we can assume you won't be doing any camping during the late fall, winter, and early spring; so let's knock one third of the calendar's availability and distribute it to those other months. That means that the eight hundred dollar a month payment divided across eight months instead of twelve means that you really pay twelve hundred per month, before insurance, maintenance, propane, electricity, storage, and gas to tow it.

If you use it two weekends a month, which seems ambitious to me, every single available month, which also seems really ambitious; you'll have sixteen weekends to use this thing per year. Sixteen weekends is thirty two days. It's costing you ninety six hundred per year to own the thing before insurance, maintenance, propane, electricity, storage, and the vehicle and gas to tow it.

The proposition of owning one of these things means that in the most optimistic of scenarios that you will be paying $300 per night … to camp. I don't know about you, but my wife would much prefer to stay in a nice hotel where she can use the pool or take a bubble bath, rather than crapping into a porta-toilet and freezing her ass off all night.

The numbers do not add up for owning one of these things, especially if you buy new, and it doesn't get much better if you buy used, unless the thing is your primary residence. In that case you're in for an entirely different lifestyle than the one they put in the brochure. Instead of waking to the sunrise in picturesque meadows, you probably spend a significant amount of your time in Walmart parking lots wondering why you set your life up so that the toilet in the Walmart bathroom is superior to all of your available options.

If a camping trip sounds fun and you don't want to rough it the old fashioned way, preferring to treat your family to an exceptional adventure that is hard to achieve in any other way, Rent an RV. Paying fifteen hundred a week seems like a lot, until you do the math on owning one yourself. Insurance is even included in your rental, I didn't even include it in the example above because you can tell it's a horrible value even without adding in all the ancillary costs.

Doing a trip like that once, or once a year will be a fun adventure the whole family will enjoy. This would be opposed to trying to get your family to go camping every other weekend so you can try to reclaim some of the value you shell out to the damn thing every month, and still take a bath on the deal. The only thing less realistic would be thinking that anyone will ever take a bath in the tiny tubs they come with.

In terms of the value proposition, the same goes for boats. Be the big spender and pay the big ticket price to rent the few times of a year you actually have time to do it. Owning will never save you money unless you intend to redefine your life and live in a camper or on a boat.

Remember, a boat is a hole in the water that you pour money into. Also, it's better to be on your boat with a drink on the rocks, than to be in the drink with your boat on the rocks.

You're not Fooling Anyone

If you're trying to climb the status ladder and rise to a higher position, I don't blame you. I think that's a pretty basic human ambition. Even lobsters want to attain the highest rung they can in their simple and primitive little lobster hierarchies. The thing is, you're not going to be able to fool anyone, that is except for the people that are trying to fool you. In fact, you could have some success fooling other fakers because they don't understand real wealth the way wealthy people do, just like you don't.

Likewise, they will be fooling you because, if you're faking, you also won't understand real wealth, and will be compromising your ability to become wealthy because you can't make peace with the station that you actually exist in.

So it will be all the fakers together faking for each other, stressing about how to maintain the old fakes and how to fake the new fakes; all while actual wealthy people can see perfectly exactly what's going on.

They've already achieved the type of wealth where they are not stressed about the purchase of a travel trailer or a boat or a beach house, or a small plane. They don't have to fake it because they used their money wisely early on and it's since compounded to make them wealthy enough that it hardly matters what they spend their money on now.

I keep saying that wealthy people are not the target market for this book, mostly because they already know this stuff. Maybe they'd read it just for fun, for some validation to see if the younger generation gets it, or if the culture and perhaps the entire species is completely doomed by the emerging social media tic-tok calamity that turned our wonderful society our elders helped build and protect into a rude collection of a bunch of social media obsessed vape zombies with no apparent purpose except to squander their inheritances on a never ending quest of self indulgence and flagellant self involvement.

Many people don't want to accept their station in life. This must be because they think their station is permanent, which in the US and most developed countries, it is not. They might think that not being able to own a boat makes them poor. It does not. We are not in a caste system like they have in India. This is the USA baby! Your station is temporary, based on your willingness to do the things you have to do to change it.

It's not easy and they don't hand it out. Actually, you're competing with every other person in your station, and those fast approaching from below, for the spot above yours, so you'll have to work at it. You'll have to work harder, more diligently, more consistently, more intelligently, more creatively than your peers to level up in your station. Some people make just one of those attributes work to achieve a level-up. You have to accept where you are so that you can properly plot a course to where you want to go. Your station is where you are now, own it. Now do what you have to do to change it, if that's what you want to do.

One of the reasons why first generation immigrants do so well in the United States is that they do not view themselves as poor. They arrived poor in many cases, but their self image reflects that they are on a path to become wealthy, otherwise they would not have come to begin with. They are not resentful of their position in society, they are instead grateful to have the opportunity to be in a place where they can rise up based on their actions, regardless of their origin.

Many American born people don't have this trait because they take for granted the opportunity that is their birthright. Immigrants come here because a dream took hold in them back when they were in their home countries. Many Americans take that dream for granted because they don't have any frame of reference the way their immigrant counterparts do, seeing a clear difference from where they are from to where they are going (the USA).

If you're buying boats and other stuff you can't afford you should take a step back and look at the privilege that you were lucky enough to be born into. You're in a better position, dollar for dollar earning wise, than the vast majority of the world's population.

A construction worker in Guatemala makes thirteen dollars a day. Their ability to accumulate money is practically futile, and there's plenty of places that are even worse off. You probably make more than that during your bathroom break at work. If you're unable to make a change in your station with that kind of capital available, you're probably misspending it trying to look like you're something you're not.

The difficult pill to swallow is that it is difficult to change your own station in life, even here in America. Difficult but possible. Almost guaranteed though, is that you will be able to change the station of your children from your own if you work hard at it and constantly reinvest instead of over indulge. You can see what's at stake. Get a handle on your penchant for indulgence and your kids will have a chance to worry about things that seem less important than the things you worry about.

It's the Little Things

The Starbucks example was a way to demonstrate how small but daily expenses can add up to large sums over the course of a year. Over several years a small daily expense could amount to what could have been a large investment, eventually appreciating in value and delivering dividends into perpetuity for your estate. Every alternative to a daily expense is an opportunity to reduce yearly costs in a significant way. If you can go without, that's great. If you can find a less expensive replacement, the difference will add up over time and if you can find a better use for that money, you'll be glad you made the substitute.

As I mentioned earlier, I'm a big fan of plastic wrap. When I worked at a gourmet food and wine store I learned the technique to use it properly. The boss told me I needed to be familiar with the selection of cheeses so when I had time and I saw one I hadn't yet tasted, I could cut myself a piece, then re-wrap, weigh, and print out a new price tag to put on it and put it back. As you can imagine, my first few weeks were wonderful. On paydays the owner would stay late with me to do wine tastings. There was a little bucket to spit the wine into, but I politely declined as it was a short skateboard ride home and the sunset shone more brilliantly after a glass or two of wine at the end of my shift.

The secret with plastic wrap is to wrap your object like you would wrap a present, but with the ends at the bottom. This means, put your piece of plastic wrap on the counter, set your object upside down on top of it, and stretch the sides up and over your object until they all neatly overlap on what is now the top. Then turn it over and voila, a professional wrap job with no bubbles or loose plastic. Pro-Tip: cut the label of your cheese from the original package and place it face down before you put your cheese on top. This way your cheese is labeled so you don't forget which is which.

Plastic wrap saves food by keeping air away from it, and is much less wasteful than a zip-loc bag for example. Less waste means less materials used. That means better for the environment and less expensive. Waste not want not, right?

Since my days at the Gourmet market, I like to have a selection of cheeses on hand. Using this plastic wrap system is critical to having wonderful charcuterie plates available when a friend stops by. Stock jars of different types of olives, pickles, pickled onions, sun dried tomatoes, and peppers to flush out your plates. For cured meats, best is to have them in their original sausage shape as they keep well this way and you can thinly slice off just what you need when your guests arrive. Invest in a couple of nice cutting boards, you can never have enough cutting boards for when guests want to help cook, and a couple of good looking ones should always be handy for your charcuterie boards when guests drop by.

Have different types of plastic bags for storing food. Zip-locs are great, but they're often overkill and end up being both wasteful and expensive. Remember, the less the material, the less the waste, and also the less wasted money. In Guatemala we can get an assortment of sized bags that are the type that stores give you when you buy something smaller. They are very thin plastic bags and generally cost around thirty five cents per one hundred, depending on the size. In most cases that's even cheaper than plastic wrap and we'll use them for the boy's snacks and sandwiches for their school lunches. It's not common to see those bags in the US but they can be found online. Old fashioned sandwich bags do the trick and use a lot less plastic.

Tupperware type products generally work well and help to conserve food but my favorite are jars. I like mason jars because you can freeze them if you leave enough headspace. I also collect the jars that products come in because it's a great food container that you can give away with no remorse. I'll use little jars for sauces that I make, and larger jars for soups or anything that will pour, like spaghetti or pasta salad. Pouring makes dispensing a breeze and saves getting any more utensils dirty. I've even put my famous smoked short ribs in jars before, only because I know they'll disappear quickly because you can see what they are through the glass and don't end up with stuff on top of them like would happen with tuppers. Jars are a one hundred year old solution that comes free with the products you buy.

Plastic jars are awesome too. I can not throw out a mayonnaise jar. I'll use it in my truck to keep screws, or put goldfish crackers for the boys in the car. Glass jars are the most perfect solution for storing food except for two problems: they are heavy and they can break. Plastic peanut butter jars are best; they are cylindrical and stackable and have standard tops. They are great containers and I can't believe people just throw them away. Then in the same breath will order some sucky plastic food storage product from China, who's lids will get mixed up with all the other variations of existing lids (many of whom have no corresponding container) effectively making a challenging late night IQ test for the task of trying to store some green beans.

Those nice clear orange juice jugs are perfect water jugs. I'll buy that juice for the jug if I need another one. If you don't have a gallon of water in your car at all times, you should rinse out that OJ jug instead of throwing it in the trash. 96oz of water is a really convenient thing to have and is critical in certain emergencies, and doesn't cost you anything.

It's gotten to the point that some of the packaging is so good, you can be discerning about what you keep. I don't even keep yogurt cups anymore, unless I plan to do some gardening and need tiny pots. They're not good for anything else, or that is, there's better stuff out there now. I get it that you might find it a little low brow to stock your cupboards with recycled containers. I'm not suggesting you use yogurt cups instead of glasses for dinner, I'm just saying having a few plastic cups with lids can come in handy. All you have to do to use them is wash them out.

This one might not seem worth it to many of you but it's made a big difference for me in my life. About fifteen years ago I was traveling in Guatemala and saw a nice kit with a straight razor with a nice brush to foam up some soap as shaving cream. I was nostalgic about the kit because my dad always shaved with one of those brushes and the safety razor that takes the replaceable blade. I've since converted to the type of straight razor that takes that same replaceable blade, snapped in half, giving you two blades for every one that comes in a pack of five. I also now use shaving cream from a can even though it is more wasteful, it's more convenient and is gentler on my skin.

Shaving with a straight razor takes a bit of practice, and is definitely more dangerous than a safety razor. I like it better because I already know how to do it, and it works better when your hair is a bit longer and has the tendency to clog up the safety razors. It's also cheaper, like a lot cheaper. Nowadays everybody uses the mach10s or whatever they are up to by now. The cost of shaving is a real expense because companies like Gillett have convinced men that they need to spend at least a few dollars per week just to shave their face.

For less than five dollars I bought two cards of replaceable Bic blades the retailers buy that have twelve packs of five each, each blade is broken into two pieces that can be used for about five shaves before getting dull. I only shave a few times a week, so long story short, I paid five dollars more than ten years ago and still have a bunch left. If you spend three dollars a week, that's twelve per month or one hundred and forty four per year. It doesn't seem like a big deal, but I'd rather have the hundred and forty four dollars, which after ten years is fourteen hundred and forty dollars.

Same goes for body wash. Especially for men I see this as an incredibly wasteful practice. You're paying for a plastic bottle and the water they mix the soap with. Find yourself a nice bar of soap that's gentle on your skin. You'll save a fortune over time and you can take it on airplanes without getting hassled by security.

People are for some reason fascinated with the latest and greatest thing, often unaware that it's just a method by huge multinational corporations to upgrade the expense people are willing to pay for their everyday grooming routine. SC Johnson Wax would love to double the cost of your morning routine, and they'll spend millions on commercials to influence the culture to make you think that it's normal for men to spend on what only women would spend on previously.

If packing for a trip means a bunch of tough decisions for your grooming and hygiene products, you might want to scale your selection back. They're costing you more than you think, are wasteful on many different levels, and probably aren't making you any prettier. Stick with the basics and accept yourself for what you are. If you're a man or a woman, if you have more hair products than princess Peach, you should probably focus more on developing elements of your character instead.

This life of thrift is more a psychological quest than anything. It's great to put your money where you value it most, and it's great to be less wasteful which is also good for the environment. Really what it's about is liberating yourself from the grips of modern marketing and it's darling, materialism. The body wash isn't going to make you more successful or more attractive. Unfortunately, that's not something you can just buy. Advertisers of products regularly promise things they can't deliver. They promise you an easy way to a goal that's difficult to achieve. You want to be more attractive to the opposite sex, they say buy a convertible; I say, become someone the opposite sex wants to be with. It's harder to achieve and I can't make any promises. They can't either, but they do anyway. If their products fulfilled the promises they offered, how would they sell you more products?

They know their products don't fulfill those promises and they like it that way. The last thing they want for you is to find your partner, to experience love, and to finally be content. Content people don't keep buying a bunch of crap to try to make themselves happy. Content people don't fall for the latest trend and spend all their time working to make money to fix the things the TV says are wrong with them. The system is hell bent on making you unhappy. It's not in your best interest to listen to them and go along with what they tell you to do.

The life of thrift is about seeing an advertisement that says, "you need this thing", and having the self conviction to say, "no I don't". Not thinking, "I can't afford it" or even "I wish I could have that but I can't". Call out the truth when you see it and recognize that you don't need every new shiny object they wave in front of your face. You might want some of them, and it's ok to buy things you want, as long as it doesn't damage you financially. There's a spiritual peace that comes from learning to let go of constantly lusting for material objects.

I've Been to School for Thriftiness

In Guatemala there's a lady at the Antigua market that sells used jars. I wonder how she gets them. I was looking to acquire some jars because I was planning to make some kimchi, so I went to see this lady but couldn't believe the prices she wanted to charge. I ended up buying just a couple glass jars from her and doing most of the fermentation in a huge plastic "jar" I bought from one of the 'plastic stores'. She's able to charge a lot because they are worth it.

Plastic stores are another interesting phenomena in Guatemala. Every small town has at least one. It's plastic stuff from China. Buckets, tupper type products, the plastic bags I was talking about before, and a bunch of plastic stuff. No toys, just functional plastic household stuff. I keep thinking there might be ways to replicate these successful business models when the US gets poorer. Let's hope it doesn't come to that.

The reason I keep bringing up Guatemala is because it's a really great case study as to how to live on a budget. Average people that have a salaried position, that is generally regarded as having a good job, make about three hundred and fifty dollars a month. They also get two bonus months per year so in the end they get paid for fourteen months and only work twelve minus vacations. The point remains that they are not only able to live off that small amount of money, but often support many other people with that salary.

With that salary they manage to raise a large family and put their kids into private schools and pay for uniforms etc, etc. There definitely won't be any vacations to Maui, but they might sneak out for a weekend at the waterpark/amusement park, or spend a day or two at the beach, hopefully visiting friends and not paying for hotels.

The level of indulgence that comes along with this salary is pretty low, especially after you have about three or more dependents. There's not a lot of disposable income or discretionary spending. They have to be careful with every Quetzal (7.6Q=$1). Every trip or nonessential thing they buy is something that they saved for deliberately sacrificing on something else. Needless to say, while Guatemalans are particularly well dressed, it's not because of shopping sprees at the mall, it's because of Pacas selling good used clothing for cheap.

They've got the infrastructure to live well with very little. Since only the wealthy are in a position to waste money, the vast majority of the population is looking to get the most they can for the least amount of money. That means with the least amount of waste. That means nobody with any sense would throw out a plastic jar, and especially not a glass one. It also means the entire marketplace reflects this sentiment.

It's really easy for me to see eye to eye with these people when we have approximately the same hobby: saving money. For them, it's less of a hobby, but hey, who's counting. It's a similar interest for sure, and we've all got the bug. I prefer to express my environmentalism through my lack of waste, for them it might be different, but still leads to the same end.

My wife has stories about doing family trips to the coast in the back of a box truck on mattresses, cramming the family into the vehicles they collectively had available. Eating simple sandwiches made by the hundred and packed all together in a giant trash bag. They left the Antigua area in the early morning, back by late evening, all it cost was gas and sandwiches. Cheapest family vacation ever.

Last year we actually did something pretty cool. Somebody in town arranged a trip to the coast with three school buses. (Down there they call them chicken buses. I never saw a chicken ride the bus, except maybe in a big basket wrapped in a net bag on top of the bus, but once I did see a lady with a duck in a box.)

So it was three buses to go from our town in the Antigua valley down toward the coast and then northwest up to IRTRA, the water and amusement park that is somehow government sponsored. For transportation I think it cost 100Q each ($13) for adults and kids were free, the park is heavily discounted for the families of employees of Nestle, who has a huge factory in Antigua. Luckily that was us as half of my wife's family works for Nestle. We left before sunrise and by the time we were in line at the parks it was already starting to get hot.

We did the water park first and then the amusement park. Both of these places are world class, btw, and the affiliated hotel is beautiful with great rates for big rooms for families. That being said, I wouldn't come all the way to

Guatemala for this if I were you. It's not that they are not nice, it's just that it's the same as any waterpark you've been to in the US. It's on that level of high quality resorts, but it's not the best one in the world or anything. If I were visiting Guatemala for the first time, there's a million other things Guatemala does better that you can't get anywhere else.

Anyway, the town trip to IRTRA is a bit of an institution and it was a ton of fun. At the parks you keep running into people from the town which is fun because you can exchange daily gossip of what happened on the different buses on the way in. After a fun day at the parks we pile back into the buses, hungrily consuming whatever might be left of our packed lunches. We cheated and did it the gringo way and spent a relative fortune to have fried chicken at the venue. We also ransacked what was left of our lunch bag when we got back to the bus.

On the way home there was enough gossip to last the following week with who drank too much or who snores, or who slept through the bathroom break and had to pee on the side of the road. It reminded me of highschool band trips, but in a good way. We were all sunburned and exhausted, but for most of those people, it was the one trip they would take all year, and I was honored to go with them. That being said, the ride home was brutally long.

In case you're sick of hearing about Guatemala, you have to understand that by now it's basically part of my identity. The attraction, for me, is that Guatemalans are so happy. The perfect western response would be, "Why would they be happy when they are so poor". But they aren't really poor. Ok, dollars and cents they are pretty poor. But they aren't really that poor because they have class. They dress well, keep their homes tidy, are generous with their guests, and live honest and respectable lives with very little indulgences and a lot of hard work.

People in Guatemala spend their money in a way to have a good life, instead of buying a bunch of crap they don't need. I acknowledge that perhaps the reason they are not buying a bunch of crap they do not need is because they can't afford it, and perhaps would buy it if they could, but that's beside the point. Just like everyone is now, they are being forced by economic circumstances to live with less waste. In Guatemala, people reuse and repurpose things regularly. Sometimes it's pretty clever.

They have what they need and not much else. Mostly they are not very focused on material goals and instead go about their lives and their multitude of social connections latins are famous for. What they have a lot of are friends. There is security in this.

Their relative poverty often goes unnoticed, the main exception being, when someone gets sick. When some expensive surgery is required often family members will chip in to pay for the surgery, as either a loan or more like a gift. If it's not enough, people can tap into their social connections of which there are quite typically very many. The point is, they have each other and they make it work. They reason why they are happier than your average person of the first world is because each and everyone of them are important, if nothing else, to each other. In the west you're only important if you have a nice car.

Frugality is the method we use to make the most of the money we have, and the thing we should be making the most of is our happiness. Not fun, but it should include some fun, but real happiness. That's why we spend on our children instead of overindulge ourselves. It's more fun to overindulge ourselves, but watching our children grow up having fun and being happy makes us happy, a firm and solid type of happiness that is strong and resilient.

Thrift is not so much about saving money as it is about trying to set up your life as best you can so you can be happy. For that, Guatemala gets first place.

Change Your Mind

It's critical to this whole program is that you have enough personal conviction in the future you want to achieve, that you let go of the mindsets that are holding you in a place where you feel like you have no control. You feel pressure from the wine moms in the school pickup line to get new jackets for the kids. That pressure is not ironclad. If your kids look dirty that is something you should fix, but I've already gone over ways to procure quality clothing for pennies on the dollar.

You don't have to give into social pressures that the people that pressure you give in to. They are the ones that have the self-esteem issue, not you. It's about liberating yourself from the pressures of conformity. The whole world is completely backwards, have a little bit of self conviction to do what you think is right, not what everyone else says is.

Everyone is faking "success", everyone is wrong about environmentalism, everyone is wrapped up in materialism and conformity and they are thus motivated to get you to conform too. The conformity is driving them to ignore their own best interests, and the best interests of the planet and civilization as a whole. It's causing them to work themselves to death for things they don't need, only to impress people that are doing the same thing.

It's a hack on how humans value each other and each other's opinions that has been used by separating us from our extended families and communities to then enlist us back into a type of servitude driven by our desire to alleviate the loneliness this system has been designed to create for the purpose of forcing us to work harder than we would otherwise do. They've got us ratting each other out chasing imaginary gold stars, just like in kindergarten.

This system is technically not immoral, because it's completely voluntary. It's tragically true that it doesn't feel voluntary, but it is. You can leave if you want but it takes guts to do it. You could start living for your own interests, to improve the lives of your family, but you can expect some pushback to do it.

They won't arrest you at the border or anything like that. But they will employ every psychological tool in their vast arsenal to get you to turn around before you get there. If you're not perfectly convinced of what you want before you begin your escape, you're not going anywhere. That's what conviction is. It means you know what you know and nobody can convince you otherwise. It's not being stubborn, it's calling a spade a spade. Not everything in this world is negotiable. The truth is not negotiable. To negotiate with the truth is to create a lie.

AFTERWARD

I'd like to thank anyone that made it this far and hope that you found the ideas presented in this book useful or at least validating. I encourage anyone who found this book helpful to check out my first book, *Retirement Arbitrage in Guatemala*, as it would be the ultimate guide to stretching out your money for a wonderful life.

Just paying a visit to Guatemala for a short or long vacation will do wonders to change your views on the value of money and open up your eyes to how fortunate you are to have been born into citizenship of a prosperous first world economy. It will be the best and least expensive vacation you'll ever take and you'll walk away from it with a healthy change in perspective that will continue to pay dividends for the rest of your life.

Unless you are born rich, the nature of life is very much based in this economic realm that we inhabit. In my own life there were many important crossroads where I was compelled to to take one direction over the other based on economics alone. In this sense, real liberty is effectively a product of economics, or rather the freedom from the punishing forces it will exhibit on those that defy it.

In this way it is of utmost importance to have a strategy to avoid the voluntary pitfalls that confront anyone living in our society, to constantly absorb more and more obligation, thus subjugating your own liberty and ability to break away from the powerful boundaries of a system hell bent in motivating the most enthusiastic servitude out of every last participant.

It turns out to be an incredible superpower to simply be able to stop and say, "no thank you", to the plethora of temptation that drives our collective conformity by capitalizing on our vulnerable nature to simply want to love and be loved, as is and always was, as God intended for us.

Your first glimpse into that spiritual liberation is the love of your parents, then eventually enveloping you in contentment with the company of your spouse, and finally when you experience the ultimate emotion: the pride, joy, and love you can only experience when watching your children grow to eventually take your place in this world.

John Lennon was right about at least one thing, Love IS all you need.

Because love is all you need, and you could do without so much of what we feel is necessary these days, there is a complicated framework in place to prevent you from experiencing it without toiling tirelessly first. Once you attain love, mechanisms are in place to revoke that much needed love if production minimums are not met.

After your family is in place, there are forces at work to erode the timeless foundations that bind you together and keep you in the divine presence of the warmth that is each other's love. It is your job to defend yourself and your family against the frameworks, mechanisms, and forces that seek to obstruct your ability to love each other for the purpose of seeding unhappiness and discontent in order to extract labor; as though an evil slave master had concocted the whole scheme.

I wish all of you the best of luck to escape the matrix and to put the fruits of your labor to the most direct use possible to elevate the experiences and options of your families, so that your children might someday do the same for theirs.

About the Author

Benjamin Loughrin grew up between Lake Tahoe and North County San Diego and is no stranger to the good life. After building his Home Improvement Construction company for fifteen years, he is now semi-retired with his wife and two young boys in the beautiful Antigua area of the majestic Central American country of Guatemala. Working part of the year in Lake Tahoe remodeling homes affords him the ability to pursue his property development goals in Guatemala. His passion is enjoying his life as a husband and a father and sharing his love of his second favorite country, Guatemala.

www.ingramcontent.com/pod-product-compliance
Lightning Source LLC
Chambersburg PA
CBHW050444290526
45786CB00006B/2148